點解
Where to

梁海明博士　著
Dr. Raymond Leung

點
解

Foreword
by Rex Auyeung

As we have witnessed the many recent and sudden changes in global events where the unexpected would turn into reality, many ordinary citizens must be wondering what is going on and "Why". This is particularly true to the younger generation where they are preparing or newly entering into the workforce. It is fair to assume they are anxious; not knowing how to react and also, feeling completely lost!

By reading this book, it can offer some alternatives and provide further guidance on how one should analyse different issues. This is not a book that has all the solutions. But rather, it will inspire more thinking and help readers to form an analytical approach when reviewing different challenges and perspectives of life.

I have known the author for over 30 years and not only does he have all the right academic qualifications and technical training; his extensive work experience has given him many opportunities to communicate with the younger generation. In the years I've known him, Dr. Raymond Leung has always demonstrated remarkable insight on various issues and will offer different ways to view an issue. I would highly recommend this book to young people who are about to join the workforce or to parents who are hesitant on discussing sensitive issues with their children.

Rex Auyeung Pak-kuen

Chairman of the Council, Lingnan University

March 2017

序

歐陽伯權

正如我們見證到現今世界每天都在極速地變化中,有很多過往意想不到的事情漸漸變成現實,普羅大眾都希望知道究竟如何發生和"為什麼"。 這對年輕的一代更為重要。他們正準備或剛進入職場,可想而知他們會更加焦慮,不知道如何應對,甚至不知所措!

通過閱讀這本書,它可以提供到一些替代方案和觀點,並提供一些進一步的指導和啟發,幫助分析不同的問題。這並不是一本擁有全部解決方案的書,但它可以激發到更多的思考,幫助讀者形成一種分析方法來面對不同的挑戰。

我已經認識了作者超過30多年了,他不僅一直都有很好的學歷和技能,還擁有豐富的工作經驗,這讓他有更多的機會與年輕的一代來溝通。在我與他相識的多年裏,他對不同的問題有很好的洞察力,可以提供不同的方式來審視問題。我會強烈推薦這本書給即將或剛進入職場的年輕人,或者那些想與你的孩子討論敏感問題卻不得要領的父母。多謝。

歐陽伯權

嶺南大學校董會主席

二零一七年三月

Foreword
by Professor Way Kuo

Young people are full of dreams and expectations. They are also faced with uncertainties at different stages of their lives. It is understandable to have doubts and bewilderment at certain crossroads in one's studies or careers. During moments of worry, timely advice from someone who has "been there and done that"; or from a wise man who can "light a candle that guides you through the darkness to a safe and sure future" will truly be a blessing.

Dr Raymond Leung is such a man. He has a vast amount of experience working with young people. As a renowned entrepreneur and a member of many engineering, arbitration and construction societies, he has an extensive background in mediation and arbitration. In addition to his accomplished career, he takes time to mentor young people by contributing his precious time to teaching and participating in many mentoring programmes; and working as an adjunct professor at City University of Hong Kong. Furthermore, he communicates with young people actively through email and social media whereby he gets to know what they think about, what concerns them the most, and how he can assist. He helps young people to establish proper ways of thinking and provides views on life with advice that is pragmatic and applicable.

點解

For the purpose of benefiting more young people, Dr Leung has consolidated and rearranged the questions that he has received through his email conversations with his students into seven categories: life, learning, work, career, investment, family and politics. As the old saying goes, "wisdom comes from experience". The questions covered in this book may not be exhaustive and Dr Leung's advice may not be the only solution or be applicable to everyone. Yet I am sure this publication will be a valuable and unique reference book because the questions all originated from the students.

I believe that young people, their parents, and professionals engaged in helping young people will benefit from reading this book. Happy reading!

Professor Way Kuo
President and University Distinguished Professor
City University of Hong Kong
April 2017

序

郭位

年輕人對人生充滿理想和憧憬，又常因需要面對未知的前程、人生各階段的變化而感到困惑。在這些人生道路的十字路口，有疑問和困惑是正常的。這時候，如能靜心反思，自我解惑、尋找答案，固然可貴；如能有個「過來人」或智者，「妙語一句，指點無數迷津」，啟發靈感，則不啻是個福音。

梁海明博士就是這樣一位經驗豐富而又關心年輕人成長的長輩、「過來人」。梁博士是香港著名企業家，又是多個工程師、仲裁司、營造師專業學會會員，擁有豐富的調解及仲裁經驗。事業成功之餘，不忘培育、提攜年輕人，利用空餘時間參與教學和師友計劃，並在香港城市大學擔任客座教授。他還利用現代通訊工具積極與年輕人溝通，了解他們的想法和疑問，傾聽他們的心聲，為他們解難排惑，本著「教人以善莫過高，當原其可從」的宗旨，言傳身教，幫助年輕人樹立正確思維方式和價值觀。

為了讓更多年輕人獲益，他將年輕人提出的問題分門別類，圍繞七個主題輯集成冊：人生、學業、工作、職業、投資、家庭和國家。俗話說，「不經一事，不長一智」，生命只有走過才能了解。也許書中提及的問題，不一定人人都會經歷，梁博士的解答也並非唯一的答案，未必適用所有人，但這本書無疑對年輕人具有實際參考價值，因為書中提及的問題都是梁博士與年輕人溝通時聽到的實實在在的問題。開卷有益,希望年輕人、家長,以及從事年輕人工作的專業人員能從這本書中獲益。

郭 位

香港城市大學校長及大學傑出教授

二零一七年四月

Foreword
By Dr. Sherman K.B. Leung

A life mentor is like a lighthouse; which is essential for each youngster to light up his or her life voyage especially during the uncertain and ambiguous stages in life. Nevertheless, a life mentor to youngsters is far more than a knowledge transmitter; he or she has to acquire the life competences and qualities strong enough to exert impact on a mentee's life. Life values are caught and not taught, hence effective life mentors have to be ones who can "walk the talk".

Dr. Raymond Leung is a very effective and successful life mentor to youngsters because he can walk the talk. He uses his own life experiences to demonstrate to his mentees how to equip oneself with perseverance in developing one's careers in the ever-changing workplace. Actually, he is more than an upward-moving businessman; and he keeps on widening his career and horizons across different professions. He started his career in Civil and Structural Engineering and became a Fellow Engineer in the field. However, he did not stop there but kept on developing himself in Telecommunication & Information Engineering; and later in Legal Mediation & Arbitration, and further in Public Services, with outstanding contributions to each of the above fields. His passion and enthusiasm in life greatly encourages youngsters to keep on learning throughout life and to try every effort to knock on career doors until the door of success is opened up for them.

In addition, a great mentor inspires the smallest hearts to grow big enough to change the world, and a youngster is apt to live up to what we adults believe in her or him to be. My heartfelt gratitude to Dr. Raymond Leung for his trust in a group of F.4 and F.5 students who take Visual Art as an elective in our school, and in giving them a precious opportunity to design pictures for this book. Although their graphic skills are far from mature and professional, they treated this "job" seriously and dedicated their utmost to express their limited understanding of the workplace through their art works. In their minds, they share this verse from a hymn: "I would be true (and faithful), for there are those who trust me". And because of this trust, Dr. Raymond Leung is able to let youngsters rise to become more than they can be, which I admire very much.

Dr. Sherman K.B. Leung
Principal of Stewards Pooi Tun Secondary School
April 2017

序

梁錦波

每一個年青生命中都要一盞明燈，在人生的迷惘階段，照亮他們的人生旅程。然而，要成為年青人的生命導師，不只是知識的傳遞，更必須以自己的生命素養來感染學生，並且能身體力行，以身作則的實踐自己的信念。

梁海明博士願意成為年青人的生命導師，並用自己的人生，向年青人示範了如何在變幻莫測的職場裝備自己，在事業上不斷求進，不斷擴展，甚至跨越多個界別。梁博士在大學唸建築管理，順理成章在建築界及土木工程界發展。然而，由於工作需要及個人興趣，他在訊息工程、法律調解及社會服務等多個專業界別，均有卓越的貢獻。他以行動鼓勵年青人終身學習，多作嘗試，為打開成功之門而努力。

偉大的導師能啟發學生相信自己能夠成功，這份對年青人的信任，是叫年青人努力向上的動力。衷心感謝梁博士對本校一班修讀視藝學生的信任，邀請他們為本書作平面設計及繪圖。就因為這份知遇之恩，這班學生忠於所託，甚至通宵工作，盡其所能，以單純直率的心懷及幼嫩的筆觸，表達他們對工作世界的理解。在這群學生的內心，秉持着這個信念：「我要真誠盡忠，莫負人家信任深。」正因為這份信任，年青一代能超越自我，勇闖高峰。

梁錦波
香港神託會培敦中學校長
二零一七年四月

10

Acknowledgements

This book would not have been completed if not for the encouragement I received from many of my friends and family members. Also, this book is without a doubt, the one and only book that comes from the students at the various universities and mentees at the various mentor & mentee programs, whom all contributed to the questions in this book. They are all my students from: the 2014-2017 CIEM 5150 and CIEM 6980 classes at the Hong Kong University of Science & Technology; the Information Engineering course from the Chinese University of Hong Kong; the Civil Engineering course from the Polytechnic University of Hong Kong; and mentees at the University of Toronto, the American Society of Civil Engineering Hong Kong Section, HKSAR Trade & Industry Department and the Canadian Chamber of Commerce. My deepest appreciation goes out to all of my students for all of your participation and sending me your questions, which are now all in this book. These questions inspired me to put together this book. I truly hope I can inspire others and that my book can be beneficial to many more students, mentees and their parents and also for teachers who advise or teach in the field of career development, planning and counselling.

When I first realized I had over 200 questions from my students and the mentees, I believed there would be others whom may be interested in such questions and answers. It is important to share and spread the knowledge of this kind of information. So I decided to write this book and I explored this possibility with many of my friends who are experts in psychology, education, and parents and other students. I was encouraged by all of them to complete this book and turn it into reality. To all of you, Thank you for all of the encouragement, and I am sure that whoever reads this book will appreciate it as much as I do.

The seven different categories in this book were formulated from all the various types of questions submitted. These questions reflect the concerns of our young people. These are important matters for educators, parents and adults to recognise and consider when addressing these matters with young people. Thanks again to my students and mentees for your valuable contributions.

The answers to the questions are my personal views and different people may interpret them differently. They are by no means absolute answers and some are my personal experiences, which were used to illustrate some of my own decisions made in my life. Hopefully, such personal experiences will bring inspiration to readers when they may face or come across the same questions in life.

There are a number of individuals whom I would like to express my appreciation to during the writing and editing of this book. To my dear friend Ms. Julia Fung, for her comments on the Preface, Epilogue and Career section of this book; and if not for her inspiration to make this book so attractive and welcome by so many. To my first editor, Ms. Ho Yan Leung, who also edited my first book Hong Kong Mediation Handbook 2009; and for her help on editing the English version of this book. Ho Yan's experience in editing has made this book lively and suited for our young people. To Ms. Connie Leung, the President of Rotary E-Club of District 3450 (2016-2017) for introducing me to the Stewards Pooi Tun Secondary School and giving this book more appeal to our young people. Which brings me to give my deepest thanks to the seven students of Stewards Pooi Tun Secondary School as they were selected to participate in the creation and drawing of the cartoon figures, which makes this book more appealing to youngsters. Many thanks to their teacher, Ms. Cindy Chan Yin Ming and Vice Principal, Ms. Agnes Ngai Wai Ling for their contributions, and the many hours spent commenting and amending the cartoons for this book with the students. Many thanks also to their Principal, Dr. Sherman Leung Kam Bor who was kind enough to personally comment on all the drawings and also wrote a Foreword for this book. In addition, I must thank my dear friends, Mr. Rex Auyeung Pak Kuen, Chairman of the Council of the Lingnan University and Professor Way Kuo, President and University Distinguished Professor of the City University of Hong Kong, who both wrote a Foreword for this book. All these endorsements by educators highlight and indicate this book can be used as a reference book on career development and planning, for which I am truly grateful for and I thank you for all your support. I would also like to thank Ms. Eva Rao for her efforts and hard work on the Chinese version of the book as she provided me with an excellent framework for the final Chinese version.

One person who requires a special mention where I must express my gratitude to is my mother, Ms. Tang Yuk Woon. She was a primary school teacher, an educator and a businesswoman. She devoted her life towards her family without recourse. She also put a lot of pressure on me to excel myself during my early school years. While I did not appreciate her at all when I was young, it was because of her teaching that makes me try to do my best in all things. This has made me to be who I am today. Therefore, I need to thank her for this. I am sure she will be proud to see the completion of this book. It is most regretful that she left us during my writing of the final chapter of this book. So I dedicate this book to my mother, in loving memory of her. Thank you Mom.

Last, but not the least, I must thank my wife, the Hon. Dr. Ann Chiang Lai Wan; for her encouragement and despite having a busy schedule, she even offered to edit my work while I was writing this book. This shows her passion and desire to help the youngsters of our future. Ann, I'm honoured and thank you for your good intentions, as I'm sure your time can be better spent on helping the youngsters of Hong Kong under a different capacity. I also hope my daughter, Ms. Cheryl Wing Yan Leung will benefit from reading this book. As I have said in this book, most children will not discuss their questions about life with their parents. This also applies to my daughter, so when this book is published, I trust this book will provide her with some insights and prepare

點
解

her for the future days ahead.

Thank you once again to all of you mentioned above. I am sure all who read this book will appreciate your efforts and encouragement. No words can express my sincere gratitude to you all. Thank you.

Dr. Raymond Hai Ming Leung

致謝

這本書如果沒有朋友們和家人的鼓勵是不可能完成的。有來自不同大學的同學和不同導師/員計劃的學員參於了本書的問題搜集，他們是香港科技大學2014-2017年 CIEM 5150和CIEM 6980兩門課程的學生，香港中文大學信息工程科的學生，香港理工大學土木工程科的學生，加拿大多倫多大學，美國土木工程師學會香港分會，香港政府工貿署，以及加拿大香港商會的學員計劃的學員，非常感謝你們參與本書的問題搜集。我希望這本書能對更多的學生，學員和他們的父母有所幫助，甚至於現任負責生涯規劃的教師也可以從這些問題中得到一些啟發。

當我第一次意識到各學生和學員問我有超過200條問題時，我相信應還有其他人可能會對這些問題和答案感興趣，知識共享是極為重要的，所以我最後決定寫這本書。我也和我的朋友們，其中有心理學家、教育界人士、家長和學生們探討這些問題，他們的答案都是正面的，使我備受鼓舞，最終使我完成這本書，謝謝你們！我相信無論是誰閱讀到這本書都會感受到你們對我的所有鼓勵。

本書的七個不同的篇章來自學生和學員不同類型的問題。這些問題反映到我們的年輕人所關注的事物。對於教育工作者，家長和成年人來說，也可協助他們考慮如何去解決年輕人的問題。學生和學員們，再次感謝你們。

書中的答案全是我個人對這些問題的看法，不同的人可以有不同的觀點和解讀，這些絕對不是唯一的答案。我也通過本人的經歷

點
解

來闡述了我在人生中的一些決定，希望可以激勵讀者更好地來欣賞這本書。

這本書的編寫和編輯，我感謝我親愛的朋友馮月珊女士給這本書的序言、結語和職業部分的評論，她的靈感賦予這本書更多吸引力，並受到很多人的歡迎。我的第一本書"香港調解手冊" 2009的主編梁可欣女士全力幫助我編輯了這本書的英文版本，她的編輯和修改使本書更顯活潑，適合我們的年輕人。關於這本書的吸引力，我還要感謝梁穎雯女士，第3450區網上扶輪社社長（2016-17年），向我推薦了香港神託會培敦中學，7名學生被選中參與了創作這本書的各篇卡通人物的繪畫，使書籍對青少年更有吸引力，我感謝你們，還有你們的視藝科主任陳燕明老師以及副校長倪偉玲女士，你們也給予我很大的幫助，你們花了好幾個小時來評論和修改這本書的卡通人物圖紙，感謝燕明主任和偉玲副校長。校長梁錦波博士也親自對所有的圖紙進行了評論，並撰寫了這本書的前言，謝謝錦波校長。此外，我多年的好友嶺南大學校董會主席歐陽伯權先生，及香港城市大學校長和大學傑出教授郭位博士也為本書寫了前言，我非常感謝你們的全力支持。這些教育界人士的認同為本書增添色彩，也使本書更適用為生涯規劃的參考書。我還要感謝饒玉霞女士在中文版的努力，她為中文版提供了非常好的框架，謝謝小饒你勞心勞力的貢獻。

我的母親梁鄧玉媛女士也是我一定要感謝的人。她是一位小學老師，教育工作者和商人，她一生無私地為家人作出犧牲。她在我年幼時給我很多學業壓力，我一直感覺得不到認同。但這些壓力使我凡事要求自己做到最好，有始有終，也因此成為了今天的我。我在此要特別感謝她。我很相信如果她看到這本書，她會以此為榮。可惜在我即將完成這本書之前，她離我們而去，所以我也希望以本書記念她的貢獻,親愛的母親,多謝妳。

最後,也極為重要的是,我要感謝我的太太蔣麗芸博士。她原本打算犧牲自己的休息時間來幫我策劃編輯這本書,因為她一直以來都希望幫助年輕人。麗芸,感謝你希望幫助我,但我不希望占用你在這方面過多的時間,因為你還要用不同的身份和時間去幫助全港的市民。我也希望我女兒梁詠欣能從這本書中受益,正如我在書中所說,大多數孩子不會和他們的父母一起討論他們的人生問題,這句話也適用於我的女兒,但是我相信這本書也可以提供到一些對於她未來困惑的啟發。

對你們所有的人,我再次衷心感謝你們。我相信你們的努力和鼓勵將受到所有讀者的欣賞。我對你們的感激無以言表,只能再次說聲多謝。

梁海明博士

About the Author

Ir. Prof. Raymond Hai Ming Leung is a qualified engineer of FICE, FASCE, FHKIE, PEng, RPE, FHKICM, FHKIArb, CEng, and SMIEEE. He holds a Masters in Construction Management from the University of Toronto, Canada; a PhD in Information Engineering from The Chinese University of Hong Kong; and he is the inventor of two trademarks in Optical Printed Circuit Board (PCB). He is currently the Chairman & Chief Executive Officer of C & L Holdings Ltd. involved with contract advisory and investment work as well as dealing in China business. He is an Independent Non-Executive Director (INED) of China State Construction Int'l Holdings Ltd (3311). Dr. Leung also serves in various organisations e.g. Heung Yee Kuk Councillor, Standing Committee Member of the Chinese Chamber of Commerce, Hong Kong Real Property Federation Advisory Councillor, Governor and Past President of the Canadian University Association. He has 40 years of experience in both property and construction sectors and worked for major corporations including Gammon Construction, Sun Hung Kai Property, Wharf (China) and Dragages. He also has extensive experience in the telecommunication and information engineering sectors, including fiber optics (CERNET) and wireless (Smartone) networks construction. He initiated various research projects in Optical Printed Circuit Board.

Dr. Leung is an experienced Mediator and Arbitrator. He has

been involved in a large number of mediation and arbitration cases related to Construction, Property, Import/Export, Telecommunications, Intellectual Property, Trademark, Loan Agreements and Shareholders' Disputes. In addition, he holds the position as Founding President and Governor of the Hong Kong Mediation Centre, Past President of Hong Kong Institute of Arbitrators, General Editor & Author of six books namely: Asia Mediation Handbook, 2015; 調解實務與技巧, 2014; 調解通鑒, 2012; China Arbitration Handbook, 2011; Hong Kong Mediation Handbook, 2009; Hong Kong Mediation Handbook 2nd edition, 2014; and Co-Author of the Mediation and the Legal Practitioner, 2011 (in the First Special Release to the 2011 Hong Kong Civil Procedure). He is also a Member of the Steering Committee and Accreditation Subcommittee on Mediation for the HKSAR Department of Justice and the Working Parties for the Reform of the Law of Arbitration in Hong Kong and the Mediation Bill. He has been involved in various roles for 16 arbitration and mediation organisations within China as well as overseas; Panel of Mediators of HKIAC, HKMC, HKMAAL, HKICM, Assessors of HKMC and HKMAAL, Panel of Arbitrators of HKIAC, CIETAC, BAC, WAC, GZAC, SZAC, Expert Witness & Adjudicator of HKICM and Member of HKSAR Business Facilitation Advisory Committee.

Further to his vast professional background, Dr. Leung has been teaching and conducting research at the Hong Kong University of Science and Technology (HKUST) since 2010. He is an Adjunct Professor of the Civil Engineering Department at HKUST and is currently teaching a University Prized Master course on 'Dispute Resolution for Engineers'. He has carried out research projects annually with 5 research graduate students on construction management subjects. He is on the Editorial Advisory Panel of the Institution of Civil Engineer's International Journal on Management, Procurement and Law and a Reviewer for the City University of Hong Kong Press Ltd. He is also the Chairman of the Departmental Advisory Committee at City University of Hong Kong Department of Chemistry. He has been involved with many Mentor/Mentee programs for over 10 years with HKUST, American Society of Civil Engineers (HK), The Polytechnic University, The Chinese University of Hong Kong, the Civil Engineering Department of the University of Toronto, Trade and Industry Department of the HKSAR, and the Canadian Chamber of Commerce. He was previously an Adjunct Professor of the School of Law at City University of Hong Kong. He actively continues to be involved in the areas of education and knowledge sharing with the young people and organisations in Hong Kong.

作者簡介

梁海明教授是英國工程師學會，美國工程師學會，香港工程師學會，加拿大工程學會的資深工程師，香港營造師學會資深營造師及原會長，香港仲裁司學會資深會員及原會長，美國電子學會資深會員等，擁有加拿大多倫多大學建築管理碩士學位，香港中文大學信息工程博士學位。他發起多項光學電路板研究項目，並且是兩個光學印刷電路板商標的持有人。他目前是仲良控股有限公司的主席兼首席執行官，從事中國業務，合同諮詢和投資，也是中國建築國際控股有限公司（3311）獨立非執行董事，同時他還是很多組織機構的代表，包括香港中華總商會常董，香港鄉議局議員，香港房地產協會監事和加拿大同學會監事及原會長等等。他在過去40年中曾在多間大型企業工作，包括金門建築，新鴻基房地產，九龍倉(中國)及寶嘉建築等房地產及建築公司。他有豐富的電信和信息工程經驗，包括光纖網絡（教育網）和無線網絡（數碼通）等的建設。

梁博士具有豐富的調解及仲裁經驗，曾處理過多項涉及建築、房地產、進出口、電訊、版權及股權爭議之調解及仲裁個案。梁博士除了曾經是國際專家學會、香港和解中心創會會長及香港仲裁司學會原會長之外，還編寫及出版了六本書:《Asia Mediation Handbook》2015，《調解實務與技巧》2014，《調解通鑒》2012，《China Arbitration Handbook》2011，《Hong Kong Mediation Handbook》2009，《Hong Kong Mediation Handbook》第二版本2014，以及主編首本雙語香港和解期刊。他曾是香港法律改革委員會按訴訟成果收費小組委員會成員及律政司仲裁法案小組委員，現為律政司的調解專責小組委員，同時擔任中國和海外共十六個

點
解

仲裁和調解組織的仲裁員及調解員，如香港國際仲裁中心，香港營造師學會、中國貿仲、北仲、武仲、廣仲、深仲等等，也是香港和解中心和香港調解資歷評審協會的調解員和調解評估員，以及香港特別行政區財政司的方便營商咨詢委員會成員。

除此之外，他也是香港科技大學之土木及環境工程學系客座教授，任教"工程師糾紛處理"碩士課程。他每年都會帶領五名碩士研究生研究建築管理方面的題目。他也是英國工程師學會管理，採購，及法律國際期刊和香港城市大學出版社評審委員。香港城市大學化學系顧問委員會主席，亦曾擔任香港城市大學法律學院客座教授。他在過去的十多年參與多個香港科技大學、香港理工大學、香港中文大學、加拿大多倫多大學工程系、香港政府工業貿易署、美國工程師學會香港分會、及加拿大商會的導師/學員計劃。他多年來一直積極參與香港年青人教育，與學生和不同的團體作經驗分享。

Table of Contents

目錄

Preface

It is wonderful to be young. When we are young, we will likely encounter issues or situations that are critical and difficult to handle. We seldom go to our parents for guidance because of preconceived ideas. In most cases, we will not go to our teachers for advice either. We always want to show that we can solve the problems we face in life on our own and display independent views to tell them that we are quite grown up already. We are no longer mummy's boy or daddy's girl. We often feel that our parents would never quite understand what issues or priorities are important to us in life.

What can one do when one encounters an issue that affects one's life? Most young adults will consult their trusted friends, colleagues, or love ones. They are mostly in the same age group. The solutions found can be right or wrong as these "young advisors" lack the experience and knowledge in life to help another solve the problems put forward to them. They can only come up with solutions that are devised from the best of their knowledge. Some of these solutions may be negative in nature and may cause depression, and in extreme cases can lead to illegal actions or even suicide. Some answers only provide a temporary solution, which cannot resolve the problem put forward but rather might bring further frustration. Some fortunate few may resolve their issues in a positive and progressive manner.

I am fortunate enough to have an interesting and rewarding career and I am still able to spare enough time to be involved and to participate in teaching on many mentorship programs with various organisations. This gives me the opportunity to meet numerous students/ mentees. All my students and mentees are University undergraduates in their final year or graduate students. Most of them are working full-time and studying part-time programs. These young people are in their early 20's to 30 years of age. They all work very hard and are trying to create a career of their own and forming a family that fits their needs. They have all encountered issues that have significant impact on their future life. They have posed some difficult questions that require deep contemplation and reflection.

For the past few years, I have tried my best to answer some of these questions from different students and mentees and before I knew it, I accumulated over 200 questions on life in general. It is by no means a comprehensive and all-inclusive list of questions and answers but I think it does provide a good indication of what are some of these hard-working students and individuals are facing in life today. The answers are not intended to be absolute but hopefully, they will inspire young minds to reach different solutions in a positive manner.

It is my aim to present these original questions from these students with only minor changes for easy reading. Responses to these questions are intended to be additional references for students to apply at their own discretion. I have also included some of my personal experiences to illustrate some of the points I make in my responses. I believe that it is important to create the right mindset for each individual young mind. Everyone can be successful when one has the right mindset. I also present the questions in both English and Chinese to give an alternative choice in language for the reader. It is with great pleasure that I was able to collaborate with a high school and have them participate in the cover and graphic design within this book. These graphics are original illustrations drawn by high school students and I trust they will add more colour to the book, making it more fun to read.

This book is arranged under seven different categories: Life, Learning, Work, Career, Investment, Family, and Country. These categories are formulated from all the questions submitted. Each category has its own section summary for easy reference. This is a book for the younger generation, but it is also a book for their parents too.

After reading this book, I hope we can all appreciate some of the difficulties the younger generation are facing in life today, and through this self-appreciation, we should have a better understanding of our younger generation. Hopefully, the responses and answers in this book will inspire them to embark on a more positive and constructive way of life, and that they are able to better serve the community one day.

To all parents, I believe they may wish to understand their

children more and want to find out what are the questions that often puzzle the younger generation of today. This book will provide some of these questions and answers, which are surely by no means exhaustive. There are different views and perspectives to every matter but as long as it can inspire a positive and constructive attitude towards life in our young, I think this is sufficient for the purposes of this book.

This book can be used as a reference guide to students, teachers and parents. It can also be used as a textbook for a course on life planning. As this is a general book, it has no cultural or territorial limitations. It is my wish that all young people can benefit from the positive and constructive thinking of this book, and that they may lead a more fulfilling, happier and healthier life, enjoying every moment of it to the fullest.

Dr. Raymond H.M. Leung

點
解

前言

年青是人生最美好及一切蓄勢待發的時段。年輕人面對未知的前景有一連串的疑問，在尋找方向的過程中，有些年輕人為避免父母的主觀意見或想證明自己可以在生活中自我解決這些問題，以顯示自己長大了，再不是媽媽的小孩或爸爸的寶貝而往往不會向父母老師或長輩求證，年輕人總覺得父母永遠不能理解他們生活中最重要和優先的問題。

遇到人生問題的時候該怎麼辦？大多數年輕人會自尋答案或諮詢他們認為可信任的朋輩。基於同一年齡層的朋輩可能同樣地缺乏人生經驗及知識，因此有些答案只是治標不治本，不單止問題不能解決，還可能會帶來更大的挫敗感。當然亦有些幸運的年輕人能尋求到積極和正面的答案去解決問題。

我很幸運在職業生涯空餘時間能參與教學工作及師友計劃，而令我接觸到更多的年輕人和畢業生。我的學生多是即將畢業的大學生或剛涉足社會的研究生，年齡是二十多至三十歲左右，正為自己的事業及創造未來家庭努力的時候；他們亦面對一些可能會對未來人生進程產生重大影響而必需要深思熟慮的問題。

過去幾年，我一直以電郵解答他們的問題，不知不覺地已累積超過200多條問與答。當然，這絕對不代表年輕人面對的所有問題，但相信已為這些正在努力工作的年輕人提供了一些未來生活導向的參考材料。我的答案不是絕對的，但我希望它能激勵年輕人以

點
解

積極的思維來找出人生中不同問題的解決方案。

書中揀選的200多條問題基本上都是來自這些年輕人的原始問題。在回答過程中，為證明書中的一些觀點我也引述了關於我本人的一些實踐經驗。整體而言，我認為一個人在考慮問題時擁有正確的思維和態度是成功之基石。書中的問與答分別用英文和中文撰寫，以方便一些年輕人可能只想閱讀其中一種語言。我同時也邀請了一所高中學校的學生為這本書作平面設計和繪圖，以令內文圖文並茂，增添閱讀樂趣。

這本書分為七個不同主題，包括年輕人的人生、學習、工作、職業、投資、家庭和國家。這些類別是從學員提交的問題中製定出來的，每個主題都有我的個人分享以供參考。這是一本年輕人的書，也是送給家長及年輕人的書。

閱讀本書後，希望大家可以體會到年輕人在人生中的一些問題，通過這些問題，我們可以更加理解當代的年輕人，從而更好的關心他們。希望通過本書的答案能啟發、鼓舞年輕人以更積極正面的態度走上成功的人生道路和以後更好地貢獻社會。

我相信父母可能想更多的瞭解孩子們在人生中的問題，這本書可以提供父母作為參考。當然，問題與答案總不能詳盡，各人的觀點與角度亦有所不同，但只要它能為年輕人提供到積極和正面的態度，我認為這就已經足夠了。

本書歡迎作為學生、教師和家長的參考資料，也可以用作生涯規

劃課程的教科書。這是一本概括性的書，因此它沒有任何文化上
或者地域性的限制。我希望所有年輕人能從這本書得到積極及正
面思維而有所受益。不論是在今天還是未來的人生路上，活得更
充實、更健康、更愉快！

梁海明博士

Life
人生

Life brings many questions and challenges. One needs to face these challenges head on to achieve one's objectives in life. Many young people have questions about life and one needs to have a positive and pro-active approach towards such questions to walk the path of life.

人生過程中總會有許多問題和挑戰，每個人都需要面對這些挑戰，才可達到人生目標。很多年輕人在生活中都會遇到各種各樣的阻礙和困難。只要有正面、積極和主動思維來面對而不要沮喪，一定可以走出光明的人生道路。

It shall not come as a surprise that this section comprises of the most questions asked by young people. Many of them reach a crossroad where they seek answers to some of these questions. We address needs and make decisions that may affect the rest of our lives. Questions relate to how one can balance life between work and family, work and interest, achievement and rest, and time management etc. Preparation for the future is important to many of us. Often, the driving force to work harder is the next challenge we may face or our dreams to achieve our purpose in life. How one deals with another's views and how one expands their social network can also be important issues that many young people are concerned with in our ever-growing society.

人生這個部分的問題是我們年輕人問得最多的，這一點實在不奇怪，因為當他們面對十字路口時，要做出一定的選擇，而這些選擇的結果可能會影響他們的一生。問題包括了如何平衡工作與家庭，工作和興趣，事業成就和休息，時間管理等等。人生未來關鍵在於做好準備，人生的挑戰、夢想和人生目標經常是年輕人努力工作的驅動力。當然，如何面對他人的意見，如何擴大自己的社交網絡對許多當下的年輕人來說也同樣至關重要。

Life experience will accumulate over a lifetime. Some answers may not be obvious but will prove itself with time. There are always many different approaches to address a single issue. One needs to consider the different approaches before making a final decision in life. I have gone through different stages of my life and was lucky enough to experience different industries and different professions. Therefore, I hope that I can share some of these experiences with you so that you can take them into account while making life decisions of your own. Life is short and precious. We should not waste time on issues that have little affect on your life and must pursue on the purpose of life.

人生經驗是隨着時間積累的，有一些答案現在可能不太明顯，但隨着時間可以證明是正確的，每一個問題都可以有許多不同的解決辦法。在人生路上，要詳細考慮不同的方法，才能作出最終決定。我在人生的不同階段中也很幸運地參與不同的行業和不同的專業，因此我希望可以與大家分享一些這方面的體驗，以便在你作出決定前能有所啟發。人生短暫而珍貴，我們不要浪費時間在這些細枝末節的事情上，而是應該堅定地追求自己的人生目標。

Questions & Answers:

問題和答案:

1. If you had a time machine, what time of your life would you go back to and why?

   如果你有一臺時光機，你想要回到人生什麼時間？為什麼？

I will not go back to my past. It was hard work. I enjoy the present time and treasure every moment of my life. I believe that there is always a better tomorrow for me. Why would I want to go back when I can progress better in life? I now have more experience than before and I can create a better future. I am a positive thinker and I believe in a better tomorrow.

我不會回到過去，我的過去很艱苦，花費了很多努力才達成我的目標。我享受現在並珍惜生命的每一刻時光，我相信未來會比以前更好，為什麼還要回到過去呢？我現在比以前經驗豐富，可以創造更好的明天，我的思路是積極的，並且永遠相信未來會更美好。

2. Which animal would best represent your personality? Why?

你會用什麼動物來形容你自己？為什麼？

I was born in the year of the horse. I work very hard. I trust I am really a horse. I keep working to create a better future for tomorrow, others and myself. Life is never easy for me but I make the best of it.

我是馬年出生的，我一直很努力工作，我覺得我挺像一匹
馬。我一直為自己和他人努力工作，創造美好的明天，永不
言休。人生對我來講從來不容易，但我樂在其中。

3. If you are unfortunately born with one of three common
disabilities - blindness, deafness or dumbness, which one
will you choose?
最常見的三種殘疾：失明、失聰、啞，如果你不幸的患上其
中一種先天疾病，你希望是哪一種？

I think I can accept deafness. I can learn lip
reading to understand what is going on
around me. I can see the results of
what I created. I will have a silent
world where I can focus on my
work. It will affect my work the
least and I can still work to
help others. Even with blindness
I can still function but it will be with
less efficiency.
我覺得 "聾" 還能接受。我可以通
過讀唇語來了解週邊的事情。我可以
看到我做出的工作成果，甚至我可以有
個更安靜的世界使我可以更專心於我的
工作，這樣對我的工作影響是最少的。
甚至盲我覺得仍能接受，因為這只是會影
響到我的效率而已。

4. Should teenagers pursue money or something they want to do?

    年輕人是應該追求金錢還是一些他們真正想做的事情？

We all want to do whatever we want but that is not the reality. Society has its own rules and order. As a member of our society, we must comply with these rules and regulations. The structure of our society was established way before you were born. That is how society keeps its order. We can only change the structure through constructive ideas and proper procedures. Money is used to satisfy needs. You need money to survive and to fulfill your obligations in life e.g. raising a family, maintaining a certain standard of living etc. You will need to reach a balance of both in order to have a happy life. If you have no money, I am sure you will not be a happy person. Balance is important in life. Priorities are also important in life.

我們所有人都想做自己希望想做的事，但這不現實。每個社會都有它的規律，作為社會的一份子，我們必須遵守這些規律。社會結構早在你出生之前就已經建立好了，這是社會秩序得以維持的原因。我們只能通過有建設性的理念和經過既定的程序來改變其本身結構。金錢能滿足人的生活需求，你需要錢來滿足生活所需並履行你的基本責任，比如組建家庭，維持生活水平等。你需要有兩方面的平衡，才能擁有幸福的生活。如果你沒有錢，我相信你不會是一個快樂的人。平衡很重要，懂得在人生中分清主次和先後也同樣的重要。

5. What we should focus on in our life?
   我們在人生中要關注些什麼？

Focus on the areas of your interests and work. You can aspire to become whatever you want e.g. I want to be the best Project Manager. I want to be the best Bartender. I want to be the best Chef. You will need to excel in your area of work. You have to learn how to become the best. If you want to make the best cocktail in town, you have to do research and try to do it with your best effort to the finest detail. No mistake shall be made in your presentation.

專注於你的興趣和工作，要有自己的目標。例如我想做當地最好的項目經理，我想做最好的酒保，或者最好的廚師等等。想要在工作上出色，就需要學習。如果你想在酒吧裏調一杯最好的雞尾酒，你就必須先去搜尋相關的知識而且要將所有細節做到最好，並且在展示的時候不能有任何差錯。

6. Use one sentence to represent your life so far.
   用一句話來形容你的人生。

I live a rewarding, happy and fulfilling life with a great family; and I can contribute to our society.

我擁有一個非常美好的家庭，同時我能為社會做出貢獻，活得很有意義、快樂、滿足。

7. In terms of making a living in Hong Kong, the word "living" is referred more often to "survive", than having a "life". Compared to other cities like Melbourne, the most livable

city or Denmark, the happiest country – how can I live like the people there?

關於在香港謀生，"生活"這個名詞更多的是"生存/生計"而不是"人生"。對比其它國家例如最適宜居住的城市——墨爾本，或是最快樂的國家——丹麥，我怎麼才能像那裏的人那樣生活呢？

With an open and positive mind, aspire to form a positive attitude. Work hard for the future and forget about yesterday. One can live anywhere and be happy. There are happy and sad people regardless of where you live. Happiness comes from within. You create happiness with positive thinking and feeling content. Treasure the good fortunes of what your life can bring and cherish every moment to enjoy your future.

要有開放的思維和正面的思想，為未來努力工作並忘掉昨天，一個人在哪裏都可以生活得很快樂。不論你住在哪裏都有快樂與不快樂的人，快樂是發自內心的。你可以用正面的思維來營造快樂，珍惜現有的一切，享受未來。

8. 1 day has 24 hours - (8 Working hours + 3 Dining hours + 2 Transportation hours + 7 Sleeping hours) = 4 hours of My Life. What can I do with these 4 hours to invigorate my life?

一天24小時減去（工作8小時+吃飯3小時+交通2小時+睡覺7小時）=我只有4小時的生命。我怎樣可以讓這四小時給我的生活增添一些亮點呢？

Do something that you enjoy e.g. listen to music, play sports, read a book, learn something new, relax your mind, spend time with your family, or take up a new hobby. You must enjoy your dining time of 3 hours. Try to relax during your spare time so you can be prepared for the next challenge.

做你喜歡的事，例如聽歌、運動、閱讀、學習新鮮的知識，放鬆你自己，與家人交流，找一個興趣或愛好，你一定會很享受你的三小時用餐時間。在你的空閑時間，盡量放鬆，並為下一個挑戰做好準備。

9. Can we ever have the same standard in the quality of living as Japan? They do not have domestic helpers to spoil their children and they are trained at primary school to clean up their mess.

我們可以有像日本一樣的生活質量嗎？不需要有溺愛孩子的家傭，每個人都可以通過小學的訓練自己清潔打掃。

The Japanese people have a good quality of living but the average person is poor. They work very long hours, an average of 10-12 hours every day. It is also very expensive to live in Japan. They have one of the highest tax structures. They are a country with large deficits in respect of its GDP. Japanese people take very few leisure travel trips and some only go once in their lifetime after retirement. Most Japanese women do not work and stay home as the Japanese culture is of very strong male dominance. Hong Kongers can afford to have domestic helpers to do most of the housework so that Hong Kong women can work and earn extra money.

I agree that we need to teach our children discipline so that they are not spoiled. This will largely depend on the family training and responsibility of the parents.

In addition, we only have a 15.5% tax rate in Hong Kong and we have no debts. We have surplus in our government. We can go on annual trips even during the non-holidays. We enjoy international cuisines. We embrace an international culture. I have been to many different countries in my life and I will not trade Hong Kong for any other place. I spent 15 years studying and working abroad and it was one of the best decisions in my life to come back to Hong Kong; and be able to observe the handover of Hong Kong, participate in the development of Hong Kong and China, and see the growth of the Chinese economy. It was the choice of my life and I have no regrets.

日本人有良好的生活習慣，但那裏的人平均很貧窮，他們每天的工作時間非常長，平均10-12個小時。在日本居住非常昂貴，他們的稅務結構非常高，他們國家在經濟上有很大的赤字，他們很少去外旅行，一些日本人甚至只能在退休後才能出去走一走。大部分日本女性不工作只留在家裏，他們的男子主義非常嚴重。我們可以聘用家傭，女性可以出外工作，使我們有更好的生活。我同意小孩是需要管教的，以免他們被寵壞，但教導孩子是父母的責任。

另外，我們現有的稅率是15.5%，我們沒有欠任何外債還有盈餘，我們放假去旅行每年最少都可以去一次，我們可以享受各國的文化及美食。我這一生去過很多國家但我不會用任何地方來和香港交換。我在海外讀書及工作了15年，而我一生最好的決定是回來香港，這讓我有機會感受香港回歸，參與香港和國家的發展和興建，以及見證了中國經濟的增長。這是我人生中最好的選擇，完全沒有任何一點遺憾。

10. Are the things you are doing now the things that you wanted to do when you were my age?

你現在做的事情是不是你在和我同齡的時候想做的事呢？

I have moved into different areas and fields of work that I would never have dreamed of when I was your age. I only wanted to be the best engineer in my field of work i.e. construction. Life will take you to different opportunities and challenge you with different risks. We live in a competitive world and there will always be different challenges that one needs to face. Be prepared and you will succeed.

我每次更換到不同的領域都是我在你這個年齡時做夢都沒有想到的，我曾經只想做建築行業的一名最好的工程師及營造師。但生命的有趣就在於會給你不同的機遇和風險，我們生活在一個充滿競爭的年代，永遠有不同的挑戰要面對，做好準備，這樣你就會贏。

11. During the times you feel tired or frustrated, how would you deal with it?

當你感到疲憊或者失意的時候，你會怎麼辦？

When you are tired, you need to rest. When you are frustrated, you need to keep trying and do not give up. Life will always get better. Go get some exercise to rest your mind. Then, come back to where you left off and keep going. You must keep going until you succeed. There are no failures in life unless you give up.

當你累了，你需要休息。當你遇到挫折了，你要繼續嘗試並且不能放棄，生命一定會越來越好的。可以做一些運動來讓你的大腦休息一下，再回到你中斷的地方重新開始。你必須一直努力直至你贏。在生命中，除非你放棄，否則是不會失敗的。

12. What is it like to share different beliefs with people you care about? How should I deal with it?

與其他可信的人共同分享不同的理念是怎樣的，要怎麼處理？

It is good to share your beliefs with others as long as the other person is prepared to share with you. Communication is important when you share your beliefs. You may have different views but effective communication is most important when you share views. Emotions have to be controlled and you must use a reasonable test to analyse all of the views.

只要其他人願意與你分享，你就可以和他們分享你的信念。而當你分享的時候，溝通是很重要的。你倆可以有不同的意見但有效的溝通更為重要。溝通時一定要控制自己的情緒，並且要用合理測試來分析雙方的觀點。

13. How does one manage relationships between old friends when we work at different times and places?
怎樣與不同時間和不同環境的老朋友保持聯繫？

It is much easier nowadays with so many social networks. It is good to give old friends a call or send them a message from time to time. If you are thinking of them, you should do that. If you are good friends, you will make time to meet or contact them. You manage your own time. You set your own priorities in life. As for old good friends, it is likely you do not need to meet often and still remain good friends. Value your old friends, as they are the ones who can provide you with comfort. But it is best to first trust yourself.

保持聯繫在現今這個有着很多社交媒體工具的時代是很便利的。可以時不時打電話，發短訊，如果你想念他們，你就可以這樣做。如果是你的好朋友，你會花時間去探望和聯系他們。每個人都可以管控自己的時間，也會安排自己的優先次序。作為一名好的老朋友，通常你們不需要經常見面也仍然是好朋友。珍惜你的好友，在艱難的時候，他們可以給你一些安慰，當然最終還是要相信自己。

14. How does one meet different people within the same profession or with diverse backgrounds? How can one build one's social network?
    請問如何與不同背景和專業的人士建立關係？如何建立自己的社交網絡？

    Meet different people from various student groups and professional groups. Talk to others and be proactive. Take the initiative and try not to be shy. Your friends in school and the student community can be your lifelong friends in the future. Join a Mentorship program to meet more experienced senior people.
    見不同的人包括參加不同的學生組織及專業團體，積極主動地與別人交談，不可迴避及畏縮，要有主動性，不要害羞。學生時代的朋友可以是你未來一生最長遠的朋友。加入導師與學員計劃，以便見到更多資深專家和有經驗的前輩。

15. With such a wealth of life experience already, what will be your next challenge?
    你的人生經歷已經非常豐富了，而你下一個挑戰是什麼？

    I cannot tell you what I will do in the next five years. I used to be able to do so when I was your age. I worked hard in my career and life took me to new destinations. In the future, I will probably do things I have not done before. I will contribute to the young people of Hong Kong and in China. I am Chinese and Chinese people shall not be rated as second-class citizens. As long as our country is strong, others will respect us. Looking back, history tells us many painful and hard lessons learnt. Hong Kong is my home. I will explore into new realms. I am willing to learn new things each day and I am sure new opportunities will come my way. I will excel and will also help others to excel. I will share my experience with the next generation e.g. young people like you.

我不能確定地告訴你我下一個五年要做什麼。如果我還是你的年紀，我會做好一定的規劃目標。我在事業上用盡全力，而這些努力同時會引領我去往不同的方向和目標。以後的日子，我相信我會做一些以前沒有做過的事情。我會為香港和國家的下一代做出貢獻。我是中國人，流淌的是中國人的血，而我相信中國人不可能做二等公民。只有我們的國家夠強大，其它國家的人，才會尊重我們。回顧歷史，我們已經在很慘痛的教訓中學到了很多。香港是我的家，我會探索新的領域，每天學習新的知識，我相信自然有新的機會到來，同時我會幫助他人成長，我會為下一代做更多的事情，我會向他們分享我的經驗讓他們借鑒和參考。

16. When you were young, did you ever lose direction in your life? If so, how do you find your new direction? When I was younger, I had a goal to enter into University. After I got into University, I had achieved my objective but lost my goal. I seem to be living daily without a soul. I need to redefine my objective in life and improve the present condition.

請問您年輕時有沒有曾經迷失方向？如有，請問您是怎樣找到新的方向？從小我便以升讀大學為自己的目標，升讀大學以後，我的目標終於達成，然而卻同時失去了目標，總感覺每天都過着渾渾噩噩的日子。因此我希望找到新的目標，改善現在的情況。

Everyone will find himself or herself lost during different times in life. It is up to you to find your new destination at different times. You can always create new destinations in life. You are in the IT profession now. You can think of how you can become the best IT professional e.g. the best software engineer, the best optical fiber expert, and the best wireless engineer, depending on your interests. You may need to learn multiple skills or practice areas since you do not know which field you will find yourself working in the future. You need to learn this specific knowledge. After you achieve one goal, you can create others. You can do this year by year. You can think about what you want to achieve in the coming year and set objectives for the year. You can review it annually and see how many of these objectives you achieve e.g. in the coming year I want to go to Thailand, I want to learn public speaking and I want to join a basketball team, etc. This may not necessarily only be useful for studies, it can be a lifelong skill.

每個人的一生中都會有迷惘的時刻，而怎樣找到新的方向在於你自己。你永遠都可以創造新的目標。而不同的年紀也應該有不同的目標，你現在在電信行業，你可以想如何使自己成為這個行業最出色的專業人士，比如最厲害的軟件工程師，最好的光纖專家，最好的無線網絡專家，這些根據你的興趣而定。你也可以多樣學習，因為一開始你可能未確定你自己的興趣是什麼。你要學多些不同的專業知識，一旦你達到了某一個目標，你可以再創造新的。你可以在每年的年底思考新的一年計劃，每年回顧，看看你究竟完成了多少。例如，想明年去泰國，想學習公開演講，想參加籃球隊等等。
不一定只是在學習方面，也可以是在人生中受惠的技能。

17. What can I do right now to prepare myself for my future career?
    我現在應該做些什麼來為我將來的事業做好準備？

    Learn as much as you can to gain knowledge. Travel and see the world. Understand China more and learn Mandarin if you don't know it already. Be open-minded and take interest in all things you encounter.
    學習足夠的知識，越多越好。旅遊看看世界，學習普通話，了解中國。保持開放的心態和對週邊的事情多作了解。

18. How do you allocate your time for work and rest?
    你怎樣分配工作和休息的時間？

    I try to rest well and it makes me work more efficiently. One needs to focus on work and studies. You must rest well to think right. You will make better decisions if you are well rested. You may have to sacrifice some playtime but it is all worth it at the end of the day.
    我會盡量保留充分的休息時間，因為這樣會讓我在工作上更有效率。一個人要專注工作和學習,必須首先要休息好才可有正確的思維。如果你休息得好，或許可以想得出更好的決策方案。你或許需要犧牲一些玩樂的時間，但這一切都是值得的。

19. When will you retire?
    你什麼時候會退休？

This depends on the definition of retirement. If you consider it as when one does not have to go to work from 9 to 5 each day, then I have retired since 2002. I feel that I have worked harder ever since. I think my life has become more interesting after 2002 and I learnt and did much more than I did before. Life will take you to different destinations naturally, if you work hard and focus on your work.

這要看退休的定義是什麼。如果不用朝九晚五的工作就是退休的話，那我2002年起就已經退休了。我感覺自2002年起，我有更多事做，也變得更有意思和實在。因為我可以一邊學習一邊做我想做的事情。只要你努力和專注地做事，生命會帶你去到不同的領域。

20. I am wondering if we can build a culture of finding and following one's life passion. It seems like the social norm in Hong Kong has been focusing on "getting good grades by studying hard and then you can earn more money". What about life passion? Everyone is born with their own values and goals in life, so could we get people to understand more about this? I have been involved with creating lots of related activities, but it seems that either people don't believe or are unwilling to change yet they are always complaining about this issue.

我想知道我們是否能夠建立一種文化來啟發和追隨生活上的激情？在香港社會長期以來似乎一直只注重於「取得好成

績，努力學習，然後可以賺更多的錢"，那麼生活的激情呢？每個人都有他的價值觀和人生目標，可以讓更多人瞭解這一點嗎？我一直在參與大量這方面的活動，但很多人似乎並不相信也或者是不願改變，他們只是在抱怨。

Following one's life passion is a luxury. One needs to fulfill your obligations in life before you can truly pursue life passion, unless your life passion just happens to be your chosen career. This is rare in real life. Making more money does not mean you love or have passion in the work. You can always keep your life passion along with your work. If your life passion can help you financially, that will be great. If not, then keep your life passion as your hobby. Arbitration and Mediation were my life passions but it was not considered a bread-winning or money-earning sector. I pursued these two passions all my life and I can now devote more time and energy in these areas after I had fulfilled my obligations to life e.g. to family, to my children, etc. Values can be developed and changes with time. Different goals can occur at different stages of your life. A person will always enter realms they never expect to fall into in life. One should not resist change and be only confined to certain values or goals. It is important that you focus on a single goal and do your best before you worry about another goals. You shall reap what you sow and get the reward you deserve when you achieve your goal. Set realistic and achievable goals for yourself.

保持生活的激情是一種奢侈的觀感。首先你要能滿足了生活中應盡的責任和義務，才有能力真正地追求生命中的激情，除非你這份激情恰好是你的職業，但這很少在現實生活中出現。賺更多的錢並不意味着你熱愛這份工作，你可以隨時在你的工作之外維持人生的激情。如果你的激情可以在經濟上對你有所幫助那是最好不過的，但如果沒有，那麼只能讓它成為你的愛好。仲裁和調解是我的愛好，但它不會產生很好的經濟效益，所以我一生都會保持着這愛好，在我有了很好的經濟基礎之後，我才可以把更多的時間和精力放在這些領域中。首先我必須履行人生義務，例如對家人和孩子等。價值觀在不同時候可以不斷發展和變化，不同的人生階段可以有不同的目標，一個人總是會進入到一些自己從來沒有想像到的領域。一個人不應該維持自己的價值觀不變，重要的是盡自己最大的努力專注去實現自己的目標，而不是去擔心其他人的目標。當你最終實現了自己的目標你就會獲得回報。為自己設定一些現實和能做到的目標吧！

21. Is Life only about money? Every time when I go back to Malaysia, my friends will ask me to get involved in multilevel marketing, direct sales or insurance, etc. They love to start by asking, "Do you want to get rich, do you want to retire as early as possible, and do you want to travel more?" I always get annoyed when being asked such questions. For me, I am an engineer and I want to focus on my professional development, while using my engineering expertise to (hopefully) make a social impact. I also believe that more professionals or highly educated people should opt for professional development because technical and

professional developments are factors that can contribute to the foundation and economical developments of a country. If all the smart people go to do direct sales, then who else left to contribute on expertise? How can we inspire more people to believe this?

生命只在於金錢嗎？每次我回到馬來西亞，我的朋友都會問我有關直銷或銷售保險的問題，他們喜歡問"你想賺很多錢嗎？你想提早退休嗎？你想有更多時間旅行嗎？"……這些問題使我覺得很煩。對我來講，我是一名工程師，我只關注我的專業發展，同時也想有可能的話，能運用我的專業知識做一些對社會有影響力的事情。我相信，作為專業人士，應該要選擇專業發展，因為有專業技能才能為國家打好一定的基礎，對社會做出經濟發展的貢獻，如果所有聰明人都去做直銷，誰來用專業經驗作貢獻呢？我們應該怎樣讓他人相信和明白這一點呢？

Money is not everything. Yet it is something you cannot do without either. One only needs to have sufficient money in life and should not be greedy. Greed can ruin one's reputation, let one fall into traps, cause damage to one's family, and bring about mistakes in life. You should perform your best, get ahead and do better than others, and still be able to retire early through working hard and with continuous learning. You can still travel while you are working. You do not need to wait until retirement. When you retire, you may be too old or tired to travel anyway. As an engineer, you can create a better world for others. You can build better structures. Sometimes engineers may get too technical and

點
解

forget about the soft side of the business. Our society needs different people with different backgrounds. One needs to keep an open mind and accept other's views so society can progress. Everyone has a different personality. Some are suited to be lawyers, some more suited to be accountants, while some are in sales, and some are in engineering. This depends on the individual and what he or she wants to do. Let others have a choice. Just like a good chef contributes by giving us a delicious meal, he does not need to be an engineer. So as engineers, we can only inspire people through our action. We can also share our knowledge with others.

金錢不是一切，但也不能沒有，每個人要有一定的經濟基礎來維持基本生活但不能貪婪，貪婪會毀掉一個人的聲譽，掉落陷阱，傷害家庭，及做出人生錯誤的事情。每個人總是可以通過努力工作和持續學習，展現出最好的自己，超越你的競爭對手，並且也可能可以早些退休，你也可以在工作的同時去旅行，不需要等到退休。當你退休的時候，你可能已經沒有精力或者已經太厭倦去旅行了。作為一名工程師，你可以為他人建造一個更美好的世界。有時工程師會過於考慮技術方面的問題而忘了平衡可行性。我們的社會需要不同背景的人士。我們要保持開放的思維，接受他人的觀點，社會才會進步。每個人都有自己的性格，有些人適合當律師，有些人適合做會計師，有人適合做銷售，有人適合做工程師，這取決於個人想做的是什麼，每個人都應該有自我選擇的權利。正如一個好的廚師可以為我們煮出一頓美味的飯菜，而他不一定要做一名工程師啊。作為工程師，我們只可通過行動來啟發他人，分享知識是我們能做到的。

22. To retire or not to retire?

退休與不退休？

I always wondered why people wanted to retire. What is defined by retire, or "retirement"? Isn't life about exploring and continuous working? No matter where you work, still, you are working for others. Then why do we define or determine retirement? Why not just ignore this term and use another term like "next journey"? If working is our passion, even though we "retire" from that position, we can still do lots more in other work too. If people just think about retirement, then the world will not have its natural flow. Imagine when one day a river stops flowing (because everyone retires), it is no longer beautiful.

我一直困惑為什麼很多人都想早退休，什麼是退休的定義呢？難道生命不是應該不停地探索追尋嗎？不管你是做什麼工作，在哪裏工作，你都是為他人服務的，那麼為什麼我們要退休呢？為什麼不能遺忘退休這個字而用其它字來替換，比如稱之為下一個旅程。如果工作是我們熱衷的，即使我們在這個位置退下來，我們還是可以做很多其它工作的。如果所有人都只想着退休，那是否這世界便沒有動力了？細想一下，如有一天，河水停止流動（因為每個人都退休了），那這景象也絕對不會是美好的。

The definition of retirement is always something that disturbs me. Does it mean when one does not need to go to work between 9 to 5 that one is retired? If so, one can do many things in life after retirement. If people want to stop work when they reach 65 years of age, then it is fine. It is purely a personal choice. Some do so because they can get their retirement fund e.g. working for the government or large corporations. One can always get into other interest

areas or help others. That is also a personal choice. I agree that work can be a passion but not everyone treats his or her work as passion. There is always going to be someone who keeps the river flowing in our society. Some will stop while others will continue.

退休的定義一直也很困擾我。是否一個人不用朝九晚五的工作就是退休呢？如是，那麼其實退休後一個人也可以做很多的事情。如果一個人想要在65歲的時候停止工作，這也很好，這絕對是個人的選擇。有些人可以拿到他們的退休金，比如在政府工作或是在一些大公司，有些人會選擇參於他們的新的興趣和幫助他人，這也是每個人的自我選擇。我同意你的觀點，工作可以成為一個人的熱衷，但並不是每個人都可以把他們的工作視為一種熱衷。我們的社會永遠都會有人繼續工作,來保持這條河流的滾動，有些人會停止，但也有些人會繼續的。

23. Dr Leung, as you are so successful, what is your advice to young person on how to get ahead and be able to afford a car or a house?

梁教授，您咁成功，有冇D乜意見可以俾到我地呢D年輕人，點樣向上游，點樣上到車買樓或買車啊？

First of all, I do not consider myself as successful. I make mistakes in my life and I accept them. I live by the consequences of my mistakes. One needs to know when you make mistakes and how to correct your mistakes. As I said before, there is no easy route to success. Only hard work and continuous learning can improve your situation and prepare you for the next challenge. You must spend within your limits. You should save for the rainy days as well as for the opportunity to purchase your first house or your first car.

首先，我並不認為我很成功。我接受我犯過的錯誤，在人生中也要接受錯誤帶來的後果。每個人要知道你犯了什麼錯，什麼時候去修正你的錯誤。正如我說過的，通往成功的道路是沒有捷徑的，只有努力工作和持續不斷地學習來提升自己，讓你有所準備接受未來新的挑戰。要有計劃地花費，未雨綢繆，學會儲存積蓄，才會有機會買到你第一間的房子或買你的第一部車。

24. The high cost of property in Hong Kong makes it very difficult for many young people to purchase property. Do you think young people should be a slave of property?

對於香港的樓價高企，部份認為年輕人置業無望，你覺得年輕人應否做樓奴？

Every successful person is a slave of property at one point or another in his or her life. One shall not expect to own property right after graduation. I bought my first property more than 10 years after I graduated and I also needed to pay for the mortgage of the property for quite a number of years thereafter. I had to work very hard and I needed to save up. One does not live in luxury and expect to live in a big house someday without hard work. You can start small and move up the ladder. I have a friend who decided to work in China a few years ago and saved enough money to buy property in China. After a couple of years, the property prices increased in China and he sold his property and moved back to Hong Kong. He could then afford to buy property in Hong Kong. Some young people expect to own property now without working. That is not realistic. There is no free lunch; you will need to earn it. One needs to work hard and save enough money to begin your investments. Property is an investment, which you can only start unless

you have your first bucket of gold. Some may be lucky enough to get help from parents or family, but like most people, you will need to work hard to earn it.

每一個成功人士在其人生中某一時段都是樓的奴隸。剛畢業時是不可能馬上置業的。我第一套房產都是在畢業後十多年後才購買的，而且我在買樓後的很多年還要還房屋貸款。我努力工作，努力儲錢。你不可能過着奢華的生活而盼望有一天能住上豪宅，你可以從小單位開始一步步往上。我有一位朋友幾年前到中國工作，並且儲了一些錢，在中國買了房子，過了幾年，中國房價漲了，他賣掉那套房子回到香港來，那時他已經夠錢在香港買房子了。現在有一些年輕人想不勞而獲，不用工作就可以有自己的房產，這是不現實的，天下沒有免費的午餐，你必須為此而努力。年輕人要努力工作儲錢，然後開始你的投資，而房產是一種投資，如果你沒有第一桶金，你是不會有機會買到的。有些人幸運地可能可以獲得父母和家人的一些幫助或支持，但大多數的人還是需要靠自己努力才能得到。

25. For every decade in your life, you will enter into different stages of life. In every different decade of life, what does one need to understand? What does one have to do and what should one avoid?

在人生20、30、40、50、60、70歲中，分別要進入不同的年齡狀態，在這些年齡需要了解什麼？做些什麼？避免什麼？

Different age groups will have different needs. When you are in your 20s, you do not have too much responsibility. You can enjoy your work and your life, and you learn as much as you can. You establish the social networks that may assist you in life later. You select your friends for life. You will need to try to save as much as money as possible so you are able to make investments in the future. When you are in your 30s, you begin to have your own family. Responsibilities add up with the wife or husband and children. You need to feed and support them both physically and mentally. Your expenditure will increase exponentially. Controlling budget is critical. You still need to continuously learn too. There are too many things in life that you will not be able to learn it all in a lifetime. However, once you stop learning then it is the end of you. When you are in your 40s, you may have some life savings and some life experience. It is time to know how to invest your savings to gain maximum return. Do not be greedy. Invest within your own means and ability. Do not over invest. In your 50s, you will have substantial expenditure on your child's schooling and University fees. Hopefully some of your investments will pay off. If you owned property, your mortgage will have almost come to an end and this is good news. You also need to take up some interests in life so that you can enjoy doing when you retire. In your 60s, this is the best time of your life as most of your liabilities are fulfilled e.g. your mortgage is paid off, your children are all grown up and independent. You can begin to live a life that you can enjoy. You will have your own hobbies, and do things that you like and enjoy life while you can. You have fulfilled all your obligations in life and do not owe anyone financially or mentally. You must keep up

點
解

with good health, contribute back to society and help others whenever you can. And when you are in your 70s, you need to be prepared for the worst. Make sure others can take up your outstanding work, if any, when you are gone. Enjoy your family, treasure your family and close friends, love your wife or husband who will take care of you when you are sick and sad, and do not forget to contribute to society until your last breath. Hope this gives you some insights to life and you make the most out of your decades in life.

不同年齡段會有不同的需求。當你在20來歲的時候，你沒有太多負擔的責任，你可以享受你的工作和生活，盡可能多些學習。您要建立一個將來可以對你有利的社交網絡，你可以選擇你終生的朋友，你還需要盡可能地儲錢，以便你將來有資本投資。

當你到30歲左右的時候，你開始有家庭，需要負擔家庭義務，供養妻子和孩子，並在物資上和精神上支持他們。你的開銷將會以倍增加，這時控制預算是非常關鍵的。你仍然需要不斷學習，因為生活中有太多的東西需要學習了，一旦停止也是你的終點了。

當你40歲時，你可能已經有了一定的積蓄和工作經驗，現在是時候知道如何投資你的儲蓄，以獲得最大的回報。不要貪心，按你自己的方式投資，不要超出自己的能力範圍過度投資。

在你50歲時，你孩子的大學費用會是一大筆開支，希望你的投資回報足夠應付。如果你有房產，你的貸款應該快要供完了，這是個好消息。你還需要開始找一些自己的興趣，這樣當你退休後，你可以做自己喜歡的事情。

到了60歲的時候，這是你一生中最好的時光，大部分的債務都已還清，例如你的抵押貸款，你的孩子們都長大及獨立了。你可以開始享受人生，有自己的愛好，做一些你喜歡和享受的生活。你同時已滿足了人生所有的義務，不再欠任何人的承諾或債務。保持身體健康，貢獻回報社會，幫助他人。

當你到70歲時，你需要作最壞情況的打算，做好準備。如果還有事情要辦時，你要保證你的工作能有人接手。珍惜你的家人和親密的好朋友，多愛你的妻子或丈夫，因當你生病和悲傷時她／他將會好好地照顧你。不要忘記繼續為社會服務做出貢獻，直到你咽下最後一口氣。希望這些觀點能為你生活中帶來多一些的體會。

26. In life and career, there are always problems. Do we try to avoid it or face it with courage?

    人生和事業上的難題，我們要選擇迎難而上還是選擇避免？

    I believe the one who does not give up on challenges will succeed. There are always solutions to problems and there are always problems in life or career. It is up to us to challenge the impossible. I do not believe in the impossible and I do not believe that you can avoid it anyway. Have a positive attitude and accomplish the impossible. Nothing can ever stop a confident and determined person.

    我相信一點，不放棄者就會成功。生活和事業中總會遇到問題，但任何問題都有解決方案，是由我們自己來挑戰不可能。我不相信不可能，我也不相信你能一直避免難題，只要有一個積極的態度，永遠可以完成不可能的事情。沒有什麼能阻止一個有堅持和有信心的人。

27. I am deeply interested in music and if I rate my main career as 30% of my life, then music is equal to that. Could you give me some ideas as to how I may effectively develop myself in other areas of interest?

我對音樂有很大興趣，我覺得如果我的事業佔我人生比重的百份之三十的話，音樂也會是相同的比例。你能给我一些建議如何有效地在其它領域中提升自己嗎？

You will firstly need to find a profession that will give you a reasonable standard of living e.g. engineering. You can get ahead in your profession and you can always have music as a hobby and continue to develop your music interests. For me, I was a contractor and a property developer for many years but I kept my interests in Arbitration and Mediation since 1984. I can now operate as an Arbitrator and Mediator in 16 different arbitral commissions in Hong Kong and China. Once your liabilities in life start decreasing, then you can move into your interests. You will have to make a living before you can get into other areas that may not support your bills. However, you do not have to give up your hobby or interests for your work. That may be the greatest enjoyment of your life.

你首先要找到一個行業能滿足你的基本生活需要，比如說做一名工程師，你可以先往這個職業發展，但你同時可以保持音樂，作為你的興趣並且可持續發展。我有很長一段時間做建築和房地產開發，但我自從1984年起就保持着自己在調解與仲裁方面的興趣，現在我已是16家香港和中國國內的调解和仲裁機構的仲裁員及調解員。你可以在先滿足了生活基本需求的前提下發展你的興趣。因為你首先要生存，不然不能承担興趣上的開支。但從另一方面来看，你也不需要為你的工作而放棄興趣，這可能是你人生中最享受的東西。

28. People have different goals and dreams to chase at different times in life. What are some of the goals you have now that keep you motivated and energetic?

人在生命的不同階段總有不同的目標和喜愛的東西，你在現階段有什麼目標能激發新的動力？

In my life, I place particular emphasis on the different areas of life at various stages of my life. Initially, it was in construction and then in property development. Then I move into the area of telecommunications and subsequently, in optical networks. I kept my interests in Arbitration and Mediation too and I excelled in all these areas mentioned throughout my career and achieved to become one of the key players in all these areas in Hong Kong and China. I have reached the stage where I enjoy sharing my experience and knowledge with others. So that's when I began to teach a Masters course at HKUST on dispute resolution for engineers. Working alongside myself were five Master students at the University who assisted with research on Construction Management issues. I also lead a research team, which I set up a few years ago to do research on optical PCB. I enjoy sharing with others so much I published six books on Arbitration and Mediation so far. At present, I am working on this new book for young people and I hope your questions in life will form part of the book. I hope this book can help young people and as well as their parents to appreciate that their children have questions they did not realise. I have completed my liabilities in life and I can offer my services to others and help others. As for motivation, I think it is a self-driven force. When one wants to complete certain tasks, one will need a driving force or self-initiative to achieve such objectives, no matter what the difficulties may be. This is a challenge on its own and self-initiative stems from the gratification or achievement from accomplished challenges.

我在生命中的不同時段投入於不同的領域。首先，由建築進入房地產發展，然後轉移到了電信行業，再到光纖網絡，同時還一直保持着對調解和仲裁的興趣，並且努力讓自己成為了香港和國內這些行業中的重要角色。現在，我會在不同的舞台將我的經驗和知識分享於其他人，這也是我在香港科技大學教糾紛處理碩士課程的原因，我還有五名碩士學生和我一起研究建築管理方面的問題，我喜歡和別人分享。幾年前，我組合了一個研發團隊來研發光纖電腦板。過去八年，我出版了六本關於調解和仲裁的書，目前，我正在編寫這本關於年輕人問題的書，我希望你的問題也可以出現在這本書裏。我更希望這本書可以幫助到所有年輕人和他們的家人，來多了解年輕人的問題。我已經完成了我人生的基本責任，現在我可以幫助他人，自發性便是驅使我走向未來的動力。當一個人想要完成某些任務，你會自我激發和鼓勵自己，無論事情有多麼的困難，這就是自我挑戰自己的表現，自我激勵也可以來自於完成挑戰後的滿足感。

29. What are some of the things I need to do to make a better future for myself?

為了將來更好的生活，我有什麼事情需要擅長呢？

Learn things that are related with your work. Any techniques or skills you can learn that will be beneficial to your work are desirable. Communication skills such as listening, public speaking and presentation and language are all important. You can learn anything since you will not know when it will come in handy. Remember that you can use these acquired skills and techniques for the rest of your life. Feel free to explore areas of your interests.

學習與你工作上有關聯的知識，學習所有可以提升你工作技能的知識。溝通技巧如聆聽、語言及演講技能都很重要。你要學習你不懂的東西，因為你不知甚麼時候可以用得到。不要忘記這些所學的東西，可能讓你一生受用，而不一定是現在，是未來的四至五十年，你大可廣泛地發掘你的興趣範疇。

30. What do you do after work?

你工餘時間做些什麼呢？

I do not stop working. Work is part of my life. I play golf. I read all kinds of books. I watch TV and communicate with others on social media. It takes determination to turn off the TV and get some serious work done. I trust I behave like many other people. Work is part of my life and as long as it does well to others, then I will continue with my work.

我不停地工作，工作是我人生的一部份。我也打高爾夫球，閱讀各類型的書籍，也看電視和與朋友在社交媒體溝通。有時，真是需要下定決心來關掉電視，以便認真地工作。我覺得我的行為與其他人很相似，工作是我生活的一部分，而且只要是對他人是有益的，我就一定不會停止工作了。

31. What is our purpose in life?
我們生命的意義是什麼？

One shall create a better tomorrow for others. Be constructive to our community. Help those in need. Be a contributor. Be a problem solver. Be an honest and loyal person.

我們應為他人創建一個更好的明天，要對我們的社會有所貢獻，幫助有需要的人，做一個貢獻者而非負累者，要做一個有問題去解決的人，要做一個誠實和忠誠的人。

32. What is the best influence that one can bring to society to help people and the poor at large?
一個人能為社會上的窮人和需要幫助的人帶來最好的影響和幫助是什麼？

One can create opportunities for others and the poor. You can give knowledge and educate others to help others. Education and knowledge can improve jobs so that people can have better living for tomorrow.
你可為需要幫助的人和窮人創造機會，傳遞教育和知識，知識能幫助他們改善就業，使他們有更好的明天。

33. How can we stop or reduce poverty in society?
我們怎樣可以阻止或者減少貧窮？

Improved economies create more job opportunities. Prevent corruption. China was stricken with poverty 20 years ago yet through modernization and with the right public policies, both job opportunities and growth was created. Never spend beyond your means and there will always be surplus and no one will need to be poor.
可提升經濟發展，創造就業機會，防止腐敗。中國二十年前很窮，通過現代化建設，政策配合，創造了很多就業機會和經濟發展，千萬不要消費多過自己的能力範圍，便會有盈餘而不會窮。

34. How do I know if there is a higher power guiding us or not? How can one prove this?

我如何知道是否有一股無上的能力驅使我們？你如何證明它呢？

I do not know if there is a higher power or not, but all higher powers regardless of which religion they appear from will always tell people and the community to do good and be a kind person; to always do good unto others. I will not spend time to prove whether this is true or not. It is immaterial to me. What lies ahead is what I need to address everyday for myself. I must face tomorrow's challenges as and when it crosses my path.

我不知道是否有一股無上的能力，但無論任何宗教都是告訴各人，要做善良的好人，為他人做好事。我不會花時間去求證，這對我不重要。無論是什麼指引我，我未來要面對的都是一樣，我要面對和解決我生命旅途中的所有未來的挑戰。

35. I don't want to be a slave to money but I want to have time to really enjoy what I want. I will need to find ways to raise funds somehow so which field would give me this liberty and also help me earn an ample amount?

我不想做金錢的奴隸，而是想有時間做我真正希望做的事情，因此我要想辦法積累資金。有哪一個領域可以給我這樣的條件讓我賺取更多的錢？

Everyone has basic needs. One needs to fulfill basic needs and obligations in life e.g. to your wife, your husband, children, parents, etc., before you can do whatever you want. There are limitations in life and social norms that one needs to comply with. If everyone does whatever he or she wants, then there will be chaos and no society can form. A society is people with common norms. Everyone wants to make a lot of money but it takes hard work. One can be successful in any profession or trade but you will need to be good at a particular trade. The best engineering firm makes a lot of money as does the best doctors, the biggest developer, and the best cook who works in the best restaurant. It is your choice to be in a field of your choosing.

每個人都有一定的基本需求，每個人需要滿足了這些基本需求和責任之後（比如對你的妻子、先生、孩子、父母等等）才可以做自己想做的事情。人生是有局限性的，每個人都要遵守社會規則，如果每個人都只做自己想做的那麼一個社會就會亂了。每一個社群都是大多數理念相近的人組成的。每個人都想要賺很多錢，但首先要努力工作。每一個人都可以在任何一個領域取得成功，但你必須要在這行業非常優秀。最好的工程公司賺很多錢，最好的醫生也如此，大的發展商賺取很多的錢，好的大廚也能在最好的飯店工作賺到很好的薪水和獎金。進入哪個行業是你自己的選擇。

36. I have made a lot of bad decisions in my life even though I've learned from them. How can I train myself to make better decisions and ensure they are right?

我在人生中做了很多錯誤的決定，不過我也得到很多的教訓，我要怎樣訓練自己以後能作出更好的決策，並且保證我的選擇是正確的?

Bad decisions will make you smarter. Look at other's mistakes so you can learn not to make the same mistakes in life. Making decisions require good factual analysis. You have to consider all the risks before you make a decision. The pros and cons of each decision need to be clear in your analysis. Write them down. There may not be an absolute answer but in most cases, when you list out all the good and the bad, you may be able to analyse the situation objectively. That is what we engineers are trained to do in our analytical and logical analysis of problems.

錯誤的決定會讓你更聰明，但最好是從別人的經驗中學習教訓，你要學會不要犯同樣的錯誤。做決定需要有好的分析能力，你要在做決定之前考慮到所有的風險，好的方面或者壞的都要清晰明確，把他們寫下來，或許不一定有一個絕對的答案但在很多情況下，當你寫下這些問題時，你已經能夠客觀地分析出來答案所在。這也是我們作為工程師學會的，應善於利用邏輯和分析能力來處理問題。

37. I believe for one to achieve greatness in life, one has to make sacrifices, especially family time. So is it worth it? Otherwise, you can live an ordinary, simple, happy life but no one will remember you.

我相信一個人如要取得大的成就，他一定要做出一定的犧牲，特別是在家庭生活上，這樣值得嗎？否則，就是擁有一份簡單普通而快樂的生活，但是這樣便沒有人會記得你了。

You can still balance family time with your work. You have to know when to stop. Your family is your shelter in life. You can always go back to the family when you are down or depressed. You have to know your limits in both your work and within the family. Regardless of how busy you can be, you must spend quality time with the family. Do not only communicate with friends and co-workers, you also need to communicate with your family members. They need to communicate with you too. Do not close the door of communication with family. Many people make this mistake in life. Share your life with your family. That is why they are there. Others determine the greatness achieved in life, not you. Others will judge you for what you did and whether you achieved greatness in life or not. It is not important if someone will remember you or not. It is more important that you do good for the community and help others in life. Fame is not important in life at the end of the day. Your objective is to help others and they will decide to remember you or not.

你可以平衡家庭和工作兩者的關係，你要知道什麼時候應該要停下來。家庭永遠是你的庇護所，無論在什麼時候你感覺到失落或心灰意冷，你永遠可以回到家裏。不管是在家庭還是在工作上，你要知道自己的極限。不論有多忙碌，一定要預留一些時間給家庭成員，不要只和朋友或同事交流，你要多與你的家庭成員溝通，他們需要和你交流，不要關上與家庭成員對話的門。很多人在生活中都會犯了這種錯誤，要經常與你的家人分享你的生活，這也是他們存在的原因。成就

與否是由他人來評價的，不是你自己，別人會評論你的一生
是否成功。別人能否記住你不重要，重要的是你做的事是對
社會和他人有益和有貢獻。名望在一個人生命最後並不重
要，你的人生目標是要幫助他人，而他們會決定會不會記得
你的。

38. Had you ever been inspired by some experience that had
a life-long affect on your values? (e.g. challenging projects
etc.)

你有沒有曾經受過某些經歷的啟發，以至於影響你的一生？
（比如，有挑戰性的項目等）

I am always inspired by difference experiences. Some may
be my own experience and others are from other people.
One needs to learn from others. Another's experience can
be valuable to you in the future. To me, every project was
a challenge and it always has its own characteristics and
heart breaking stories. Every project I completed did leave
me with good memories and fulfilled me in different ways.
They always gave me inspiration to my future work. This is
the accumulative experience one gets in life.

我一直都有因不同的經驗而產生的不同啟發。有些可能是我
自己的，有些是其他人的。每個人都應該向他人學習，他們
的經驗可能對你的未來是很有價值的。每一個我所做的項目
對我都是有不同的挑戰，每一個都有它的特色，也有不同的
驚心動魄的故事。我做過的每一個項目都是我很好的回憶，
並且給我不同的滿足感，它對我一生工作上都有很大的影
響，每個人都是這樣累積人生經驗的。

39. Do you think that the achievements in your career mean "success" to you? Have you accomplished your initial ambition in civil engineering?

你覺得你是否已經事業成功了？你有沒有完成當初加入土木工程時的第一個願望？

I never felt 'success' in my life. I will continue to contribute and do new things for the younger generation and our society. The definition of success is unreal. It is all relative in nature. I just believe that there are always new heights that I need to achieve and I shall continue to do so whenever I can. I never had an initial ambition. I just know that I need to try to be the best in my own profession. If I need to achieve an objective, I need to continuously work hard and learn more. I trust I am still trying to do my best at present. I suppose I have not even achieved my initial ambition yet. One's achievement is always judged by others and not by yourself. Life is a process of life-long learning, reaching for new heights and challenges.

我從沒有覺得我已經成功了，我會一直努力創新，貢獻我所能，為年輕一代和我們的社會。成功的定義是不現實的，視乎你與誰比較。我永遠覺得我應該走向每一個新的目標，只要我能做，我都會繼續下去。我沒有最初的抱負，我只知道我要不斷努力做到我在行業中的最好，而如果我要做到最好只能不停的努力工作和學習，我目前仍然是這樣，或許我還未達到我最初的抱負。一個人的成就是被他人評價的，而不是自己。生命是一生不斷學習的過程，永遠向着新的目標和挑戰進發。

40. It is common that when we grow up, our real friends become less friendly as sometimes it is quite odd to talk to someone when he or she is no longer close or interested in me anymore. How did you feel when you encountered this problem?

通常，在我們成長過程中，我們以前所擁有的真正的好朋友會變得越來越少，因為有時當他或她不再與我熟悉，或已對我的事情不感興趣了，與他深入地交談也變得有點古怪。如有這個問題你會有何感覺呢？

Friends change as you get on with your life. Different personal experiences may lead to different encounters and friends become strangers. Your friends change and so do you. You just move on with your life and life experiences. I am sure you will have different friends and encounters throughout your lifetime. This is part of life and we can only accept this. One day, you will discover that you only need a few real friends and have many good friends.

人的一生會在不同時段有不同的朋友，不同的人會有不同的經歷和遭遇，會因此而變得陌生。你的朋友在改變，你也是。 隨着人生改變，會有不同的朋友和不同的緣份及經歷，這是人生的一部分，我們要接受這一點。有一天，你會發現，你只需要有幾個真正的朋友，而同時有很多好的朋友。

41. What was the most difficult time in your life?
    你一生中最困難的時候是什麼時候？

I was extremely poor right after my graduation. I needed to pay back my student loan and I survived. Difficult times always come and go. There is always a better tomorrow. Success and failure is only a fine line. If you make it then you will be successful. If you give up then you have failed. There is no failure in life except when you give up. You only need to work hard to pull through the difficult times in life.

當我剛畢業的時候，我非常的窮，我還需要償還我的學生貸款及生存下去。困難的時候總會是有來有去的，總有一個更美好的明天。成功和失敗只是一線之差。如果你能克服困難，那麼你便會成功，如果你放棄了，你便失敗了。除非你

點
解

放棄，你永遠未失敗。你只需要努力便可跨越和面對人生中的種種困難時刻。

42. How can life be more interesting when it is boring or become a routine?
怎樣可以使我們的生活變得有意思，即使它每天都是很無聊或例行化？

You can make your life interesting. You can read up on new materials and you can travel to learn new things. You can talk to interesting people. You can always learn from others. Everyone has some good qualities and these are the things you need to learn. Whether something is boring or not is only in your mind. It is psychological. One should not have time to be bored when you still have much to learn.
只有你自己可以讓你的生活更有意義，你可以閱讀新的知識，可以旅行到別的地方去見識新的事物，和有趣的人聊天，永遠有讓你可以學習到的人，每個人都有他好的方面可以讓你學習。是否無聊完全是心理上的問題。如果你有很多東西要去學習的時候，你是不可能會有時間覺得無聊的。

43. How does one work hard when there is no pressure or no motivation? What mindset should I have for working really hard without sacrificing my health?
當沒有壓力也沒有什麼特別的動力的情況下要怎樣才能努力工作？我應該怎樣努力工作同時又不犧牲我的健康？

It is through self-motivation that one is able to work hard. You can always create pressure for yourself. You have to choose your own direction. An example is whether you choose to watch TV or turn off the TV and pick up a book to read. If you want to learn something specific then you need to read. It takes a lot of self discipline and determination. That is how I completed my PhD degree. Health is an important part of your life. Working hard does not mean you have to sacrifice your health. It is pointless to work hard if it affects your health. It will cost you more. That is why you need discipline; and you need to eat right, at the right time, and rest well. You can coordinate your working schedule to maintain good health with proper exercise, eating, and rest.

你要通過自我激勵和找尋自己努力做事的動機。你可以隨時為自己創造壓力。例如，您可以選擇觀看電視或關閉電視並拿起一本書來閱讀。如果你想學習一些具體的東西，那麼你需要閱讀。這樣做是需要很多自律和決心的。這就是我以前如何兼讀我的博士學位。健康對你的生命是非常重要，努力工作並不意味着你必須犧牲自已的健康。如果它影響你的健康，努力工作是毫無意義的，只會花費更多醫療費。這就是為什麼你需要在規律的時間吃飯和休息。你可以調整你的時間表，以保持良好的健康，同時要有適當的運動/飲食/休息和努力工作的時間。

44. People say that a successful person should focus on one thing at a time. How can one manage many businesses successfully at the same time?

很多人常說想要成功應該要專注於一件事情，你是如何能在同一時間處理這麼多不同的事情還能成功？

I try to focus on one thing at a time. I will focus on completing one task before another. I totally agree that one shall focus on one thing at a time but that does not mean that you do not have different agendas at any given moment. A good example here is that when I tried to answer your question, I do not think of anything else but answering your question and it is not until I completed all the answers before moving forward to other matters. I also think that all businesses have room for improvement. Therefore, I will not consider my career as a success or there will be no further progress.

我盡量每次都只專注於一件事情，我會先完成一件事之後才會去做下一件事。我絕對同意每次必須專注一件事情，但這並不代表你不可以在同一段時間有不同的議程和安排。有一個很好的例子便是，在我正在回答你的問題的時候，我不會考慮其它事，直到我完成解答你所有的問題後，我才會去處理下一件事情。同時我也認為所有業務永遠都有發展和改善的空間，所以我並不認為我的事業現在已經成功了，否則事業就會停滯不前了。

45. As you are a very busy person, how do you manage your time?

你這麼忙，你是怎樣管理你的時間啊？

I set out my priorities and will complete the urgent items on my list first and then move onto other matters. There are always things that need to be done, or need my attention so I will not wait until tomorrow and try to complete as much today if possible. I found that if I waited, my work will begin to accumulate and I will not be able to complete all the tasks at hand. There is always something new tomorrow. Try to finish your tasks today, not tomorrow. That is how I set my own deadlines.

我先將我要做的事列出優先順序，先處理緊急事務再處理其它。如果有事情要做，我不會等到明天，而是今天就把它完成。我發現如果我拖延的話，我的工作會累積起來，那樣我反而更難完成所有事。每天都會有新的事情要處理，今日事今日做，不要等到明天，這便是我給自己的限期了。

46. When people say that travelling can help broaden one's horizon, I feel scared and tired when travelling. Why is that?

人通常說旅行可以幫助自己擴闊視野，但我在旅途中只覺得累和害怕，這是為什麼？

Everyone is scared initially when travelling since you go to a place that is not familiar to you. But that is what gaining life experience is all about. You need to explore new ventures and learn how to deal with new matters. I am sure that you will gain a lot more from travelling. To begin, you can join a local tour where everything is already organised for you. If you go to a city or country that is unknown to you and speak a language you do not know, it will be best to join a local tour the first time and move onto individual tours next time. Enjoy it.

每個人最初在旅行時都會覺得害怕，因為去到一個不熟悉的地方，但這是人生經驗的一部份，你需要探索新的冒險，學習如何處理新的事情。我相信你會從旅行中受益良多。最初，你可以加入旅行團，其他人可以幫你安排一切，如果你去一些不穩定的國家，並且是你不熟悉的語言，你最好是參加旅行團，然後你可以在適當的時候改為個人旅遊，盡情享受吧！

47. Distribution of wealth
財富分享

Compared with the Western culture, I find that typical Asians will most likely leave money for their next of kin. Is this really a good scenario? It seems that not many of our young people focus on earning money to contribute back to the society.

與西方的文化相比，我覺得典型的亞洲人喜歡賺錢後留給下一代，這是一個好的方式嗎？看起來現在很多年輕人沒有專心地賺錢為我們的社會作出貢獻。

I think many Asians are moving away from this view. When my daughter was young, I told her that there are two ways to spend my money: one way is that I will spend it all and I will be a very happy person and the second way is that I will donate it to people in need. I had provided her with a good education and six months allowance for her to get a job. She has become a very independent woman and had not relied on me financially since graduation. It is more important for young people to learn to be independent in our society nowadays. Giving money to the next generation does not help young people to learn how to manage money and eventually the money will be gone. We need to provide for people in need. Most children in Hong Kong have more than enough in their lives and there are many others who are in more urgent need than our own children. One needs to be a world citizen and not only a family member. One will also need to be able to earn money before one can contribute back to the society. Therefore, one can not underestimate the power of having money. As long as one earns with a clean conscience, there is nothing wrong with making money. After you make the money, it is up to you as to how you want to spend it, on society or on your family.

我覺得亞洲人也在開始改變這個思維。我在我女兒小的時候就告訴她，我有兩個未來花錢的計劃，一是我花掉我所有的錢，我一定是一個很快樂的人。另一個就是我會把錢捐給有需要的人。我會為她提供最好的教學條件，並給她6個月的津貼幫助她一段時間找到工作。但她一畢業，就非常獨立，並且一直不需要依靠我的資助。為下一代留錢並不會幫助年輕人知道怎麼管理財富和適當地運用，最後便浪費了，最好的還是幫助更加有需要的人。香港的孩子已經什麼都有了，世上還有更需要幫助的人啊。我們應該是世界公民，不只是一名家庭成員。這個世界上還有很多人需要關心的，每個人都應該為自己創造財富才可回報社會，每個人都不應該看輕錢的重要性。只要你依靠自己的能力賺到應有的錢，你也可決定該怎樣得以所用，是給你的家人還是回歸社會，這完全合情合理。

48. Gratitude
感恩

I have always had a question about the changing mindsets of people, particularly in university students. It seems that a large number of university students nowadays are studying in universities because they want to earn a better income and make more money. But I think appreciating education and the community are more important. As we have been given the chance to study (mainly due to taxpayers' money from the community), it is important to focus more on contributing back to society. It seems worrying that if this scenario continues, the value of a University Education will be under-rated.

我一直對於改變人的思維心態有一個大問題，特別是對大學的大學生。當今的大學生（很大的一部分）是在為學位而讀書，因為他們想要賺更多的錢。但我覺得感激社會和大學教育是很關鍵的，因為我們很多人有機會讀書主要是通過納稅人的錢（從社會中得來的），所以我們應該明白作為一名大學生是應該要更多的回報社會，如現況持續，恐怕我們的教育價值觀跌級了。

Surely, the process of learning will determine how you perform in the future. One should enjoy his or her university years. This is where you will make friends for life. It also provides you with an easier start from others. It will give you a better living in the future. But it does not guarantee you success. You need to be hard work to be successful. Universities can train excellent professionals, civil officers, good teachers and professors but not necessarily successful entrepreneurs. Entrepreneurs are generally less logically than professionals and are willing to take more risks. I trust that whether you are studying in University or not, one must contribute to our society. An entrepreneur also makes his money from the society so he or she will also contribute back. Contribution has no limits in our society. It is for the good and betterment of our future generations.

讀書的過程一定會決定你將來的路。每個人都應該在大學幾年內享受大學生活，你會在這裏認識到一輩子的朋友，大學會為你的將來提供一個好的開始和生活基礎，甚至會為你將來的起步創造更有利的條件，但大學的學習不會擔保你一定成功，你需要努力工作才能成功。大學可以培養出優秀的專業人員，政府公務員，好的教授，但不一定可以培養出成功的企業家。企業家做事通常比專業人任少一些邏輯，他們通常是願意冒一些風險的。我相信不管你是不是大學生，都是要為社會做貢獻的。企業家也是通過社會來賺錢，同時也應回報社會。對社會做貢獻是沒有限制的，全是為了我們的下一代。

49. What are the differences between teenagers now and teenagers of the past?

現今的和以前的年輕人有什麼區別？

Not much really. We all have different dreams but we need to be practical to achieve our dreams. Give it time and persistence; and your dream will come true. We all have to face competition. Only hard work can help you to defeat your competitors.

區別不大，我們都曾有過不同的夢想，但我們需要以實際行動來達成我們的夢想。給自己多一些時間和多一些堅持，你的夢想終有一天能成真。我們每個人都要面對不同的競爭，只有勤力才能戰勝你的競爭對手。

50. What do Hong Kong's teenagers lack most of?

香港年輕人最缺乏什麼？

Hong Kong's teenagers often lack the necessary drive and initiative. Many lack the willingness to learn. Many think that life is easy. They are not prepared to work hard. Many think they know more than others. There is always someone better than you. If you want to be successful, you have to beat everyone along your path in order to be the best.

很多香港的年輕人缺乏自我激勵和主動做事的能力，他們缺乏自我學習的意欲。有些人總覺得人生是很簡單，得來容易，他們不願意勤力工作，有些人認為他們比別人懂得多，但事實上總有人比你強。如果你想要在人生中成功，你要贏到每個競爭對手和只有做得最好才會成功。

51. Do you think young people nowadays can progress faster?
    你認為現時的年輕人向上流動的機會大嗎？

    Progression is always difficult in any generation. Survival
    is for the fittest. There are always opportunities to move
    up the ladder but you will need to work hard and have
    the necessary knowledge. That is why you will need to
    continuously learn new material.
    在任何時代向上流都是困難的，只有勝任的人才能成為佼佼
    者。永遠有機會更上一層樓發展，但必須要特別勤力工作和
    要有恰當的技能及認知，所以持續學習新的事物極為重要。

52. Many elders and people from older generations indicate that
    the younger generation is not as good as them. From your
    vast experience, do you agree with this point of view?
    很多老一輩的人都會覺得新一代不如舊一代，從你豐富的社
    會經驗而言，你多大程度上認同這個說法？

    The older generation has experienced much harder times
    than the present generation. We are fortunate to live in a
    prosperous society for the last 30 years. Economic growth
    has been continuous. We did not experience starvation,
    drought or political unrest. Many older generations have
    witnessed starvation and famine in China, political unrest
    in both Hong Kong and China, people had to line up
    for drinking water during 4 days of water supply, and
    war. They surely do not want the present generation to
    experience what they had experienced. My parents came

to Hong Kong from China and practically had no money to restart their life in Hong Kong. My generation have seen or experienced what we know as poverty. Most young people have not seen this in the present day. We cannot take prosperity for granted. Fortunately, this problem only occurs in some young people and not all. I understand there are many who are willing to learn and work hard. And they will excel in their life. Young people in Hong

Kong are generally less willing to learn than their Mainland peers. They have too much temptation in their life. Their eagerness to learn is diminished when temptations distract their attention. Mainland students are more focused and more eager in their learning. They came to Hong Kong from distant places, living far away from their homes with a sole purpose to learn, and that is why they want to learn. Hong Kong students often take this for granted and many may even think they know it all or they study and learn for their parents. That is a mistake that we need to learn from. When you think you know everything, you will not learn. I always believe, even till now, that I never know enough and that is why I am always prepared to learn at any time. I hope young people will do the same for their future.

老一輩的人經歷過香港困難時期。我們現在很幸運地生活在一個繁榮的社會,在過去的30年裏,經濟持續增長,我們沒有饑餓,缺乏飲用水,政治動盪。年長的一代看到饑餓的中國,在政治動盪戰亂的時候,食水四天限量供應,市民要排隊等水。他們不想讓現在的一代經歷他們所經歷的。我的父母剛來香港時幾乎沒有錢開始自己的生活,我見過也經歷過那段貧窮困苦的日子,而我們大多數年輕人現在是沒有需要經歷的。我們不能把社會繁榮看成是理所當然的。當然,這只是一小部分人的思維,我也知道有許多年輕人仍然願意學習和勤力的,他們會在生活中出類拔萃。香港年輕人學習的自覺性比內地學生稍差,因為在他們生活中有太多的誘惑讓他們分心,其他的誘惑很容易吸引了他們的注意力。內地的學生往往更為關注向學,他們從老遠的地方來到香港,唯一目的就是學習,這就是為什麼他們很想學的原因。香港的學生可能會認為這是理所當然的，很多人甚至認為他們已經是萬事通或求學是為了父母。這是一個我們認知到的嚴重錯誤。當一個人認為自己已認識到一切，你就不會學習了。我到現在都認為，我有很多不認識的東西，所以我會隨時隨地準備學習。我希望年輕人也會為他們的未來做同樣的努力。

53. How do you differentiate winner or loser?
你如何區分出贏家和失敗者？

The winner always wins. He works hard and learns continuously. He helps others to improve. He is a good communicator. He always faces adverse conditions and come out great. He is a team member who works with others. He has a long term vision. He is creative. He is not afraid of challenges. He puts thoughts or dreams into action. He knows his limitation. He takes calculated risks. I guess loser is none of the above.

贏家永遠是贏的，他工作勤力，持續學習，幫助他人成長，還是個懂得與人溝通的人。即使面對惡劣的環境，他也不會放棄，並最終取得好的成績。他是團隊的一份子，也樂意與人合作。他有着長遠的眼光，富於創造力，不害怕挑戰。他能把自己的想法或夢想付諸行動，他知道自己的缺點和極限，懂得何時接受適當的風險。以上都沒有的人相信就是失敗者了。

54. How can I be a good negotiator?
怎樣可以做一個好的談判專家？

Practice, practice, practice. Practice makes perfect. You need general knowledge of the given subject in discussion. You need communication skills. You need presentation skills. You cannot win all the time. You have to know when to give in and when to retreat. It is an art that you need to practice with people around you. You need to know the art of reading body language and choice of words is also important.

鍛練、鍛練、不斷的鍛練，熟能生巧。你需要對議題有一定的基本知識，需要溝通技巧，你要明白到不是每一次談判都能贏，要知道什麼時候應該讓步，什麼時候要撤退。要與身邊的人鍛練這門藝術。你要懂得如何觀察身體語言，還有你選擇用詞能力也極為重要。

56. How do you know what others really think of you?
怎樣才可以知道別人究竟怎麼看你呢？

What others think of you is not important. More important is what you can achieve in life. There will be people who like you and there will be others who just don't like you regardless of what you do. Just be yourself and do the best that you can and do good to others. That is more important in life.

別人怎樣看你並不重要，重要的是你人生中可以做到什麼。總會有人無條件地喜歡你，而有些人不論你怎樣做都不喜歡你。盡最大的努力做好你自己，盡自己本份，為他人謀福祉，盡力幫助他人，在人生中這更為重要。

57. What has kept you motivated in the construction field for 40 years?

有什麼激勵你在建築行業40年？

The construction industry is a very challenging industry. It creates and constructs. It puts landmarks in every corner of the world. You can always make your mark in any project you are part of that you construct or contribute in its construction. It gives one immense job satisfaction. I had been involved with many prestigious Hong Kong and China projects in my career and I can proudly say that I contributed to all these projects. I can always talk about the projects I was involved in. I trust that I have made my mark and contributed in my lifetime.

建築行業是非常有挑戰性的行業，這行業需要有創意和建造能力。這個行業創造了世界各個角落的地標，你會在每個項目中看到你的貢獻和參與，使你得到莫大的滿足感。我在香港和中國國內工作中涉及過很多有名和前衛的項目建設，而且我很驕傲地講，我在這些項目中，我都有全力參與。這些經歷讓我有機會在這世上留下了自己的痕跡和貢獻。

58. What is your best arbitration and mediation experience?

在你的仲裁和調解經歷中，最有趣的故事是什麼？

Every arbitration or mediation experience is an experience of its own. They are all unique in nature. I had cases that lasted for a long time and I consider that as bad experiences. I had cases where I was able to help resolve in a short period of time and the parties were so happy that the case finally came to an end. I felt that I had helped the people and parties during mediation or arbitration, it gave me joy. When I meet people and parties who have been involved in a case for 8 years and I am able to resolve it in 1.5 days through mediation, it not only makes me happy but it also inspires me.

每一件仲裁或調解案例都有不同的經驗，每一件都有其獨特之處。我有過一些案件進行了很長的一段時間，我覺得那是很不好的。我也有一些案件是可以幫助雙方在短時間內解決問題，大家都很開心。我很高興能在調解或仲裁中幫助到別人。當我看到有人被案件困擾了八年之久，而我能在一天半時間內通過調解幫他解決了，這讓我非常開心和鼓舞。

59. How do I read or understand people?
   怎樣去看透和了解他人？

   By being observant and by looking at how others behave under different circumstances. Different people have different behaviour. Read their body language and see how they present themselves.
   通過觀察，觀察他們在不同的環境下的表現，不同的人有不同的表達方式，觀察他們的肢體語言，看他們是怎樣表達自己。

60. Among various fields in civil engineering, like structural and geotechnical etc., did you ever change your mind when specialising in other areas? What did you consider?

在土木工程的不同領域中，例如結構和地質等，你有沒有想過轉換到其他的領域？你是怎樣考慮的？

As an engineer, you should be able to converse as an all-rounded engineer. It depends on your job and interests. Civil Engineering is so diversified you can be in one or another specialized area at different times in your life or career. I personally like construction and I moved into property development and then subsequently moved into information engineering specializing in optical fiber. Life will take you wherever you can contribute but you must focus and try to do your best in whatever you are involved with in any given moment. You must improve yourself as you go along and be ready for the next challenge.

作為一名工程師，你需要做一個全面的工程師，這是取決於你當時的工作和興趣。土木工程是很多樣化的，你可以在人生不同的時候體驗到不同領域。我本人很喜歡建築，而後來轉到房地產開發，然後再做電信和光纖信息工程。人生會帶領你到不同的領域，但你在每個時段都要全情投入，把要做的工作盡量做到最好，你也必須要不斷提升自己，這樣才能走得更長久，在長遠的道路上，隨時準備好接受下一個新的挑戰。

My Sharing
我的分享

Life is full of surprises. We must treasure our lives and try to make the most out of it. We need to balance our lives between work and enjoyment, work and interests, work and family, prioritise our friends and expand our social networks. Nurture dreams, be prepared for the next challenge and achieve our purpose in life. It is best that we do what's right for ourselves rather than be concerned with what others think of us or want us to do. You are the only one who can take responsibility for the consequences in the decisions you make in your life.

人生是充滿驚喜的，我們一定要珍惜生命，盡量充分利用時間來達到自己的人生目標。我們要在工作/享受，工作/興趣，工作/家庭之間，朋友的選擇，社交網絡中找到合適的平衡點。培育夢想，為下一個挑戰做好準備，實現我們的人生目標。我們最好為自己而努力，而不要太過於關注別人的想法或他人對我們的期望，因為只有你自己才可以承擔自己作出的決定和後果。

If you want a happy life, you need to maintain a good balance in all of the above areas. You need to be focused in what you do. Do one thing at a time. You need to create opportunities rather than wait for the next opportunity to come to you. You have to be proactive and take initiative in your life. You have to be prepared in life. Prepare for the unexpected. One shall never give up on your objectives. Maintain your persistence to achieve your objectives. In order to have value in life, you need to do good to others. This is what life is all about.

點
解

如果你想要有一個幸福和快樂的人生，你要在所有上述的領域中保持良好的平衡。你要專注你所做的每一件事情，每一個時段做一件事情，不能三心二意。要自己主動尋找和創造機會，而不是等待機會，你必須要積極主動和有自發性，時刻做好準備，面對意想不到的挑戰。永遠不能放棄你自己的最終目標。堅持可以實現到你的人生目標，為他人做好事，這樣才會讓你增長和提升自己的人生價值，這才是一個美好的人生。

I have shared some of my personal experiences in life and on how to deal with different situations and scenarios. I hope it can enlighten you to live a happy life in the future. Good Luck.

我在這篇內分享了一些我個人在不同情況下的人生經驗，希望這些啟示能讓各位有更美滿和幸福的未來，祝各位好運。

Learning
學習

Learning is one of the most important aspects for our young. It adds value to one's life. It opens up one's mind. One will join a group of new friends who have similar interests. One can be inspired by the knowledge learnt to create new opportunities. There may be a demand for different knowledge at different times in one's life. Therefore, continuous learning becomes essential for anyone to grow.

學習對我們的年輕人來說是其中一項最重要的因素，它增強了生命的價值，開放了你的思維。你會借着學習的機會認識到更多有志同道合的新朋友，可以通過學習新的知識來啟發新的機遇。每個人在不同時段需要不同的知識。持續學習對一個人的成長至關重要。

I always find that there is a need for learning. I realised the importance of learning from the early stage of my career. My desire to learn drives me to make learning become my personal interest. I therefore have not stopped learning ever since. I hope through my personal experience I can share some of my insight with you all on the aspects of learning.

我在我職業生涯早期已經理解到學習是非常有必要的。學習的慾望驅使我把學習作為我興趣的一部分，我從此沒有停止過學習。我希望通過我個人的經驗，可以與大家分享一些我在學習方面的見解。

Questions & Answers:
問題和答案:

1. Do you find it hard to change your field of study in such a short period of time?
   你覺得在這麼短的時間內，轉換學科是件難事嗎？

   When there are needs, you just have to do it. As long as you are determined, difficulty will not come into play as you achieve the objectives you set for yourself, including things like change of field in studies.
   有時你必需要這樣做，只要你下定決心，困難與否不重要，即使轉換學科也能取得成果的。

2. Will you explore other fields of study in the future?
   你將來會不會探索另外的學科呢？

   I always explore other areas of interests. I may learn something about an area but I may not necessarily go into that field. I will explore opportunities before I decide it proves to be interesting or not. Upon further investigation, I may find that it may not be an area that I can contribute to. In that case, I will move onto something else. It is always good to explore into different areas in life. You may discover some hidden talents within yourself.
   我對於不同事物都感興趣，也會一直不停探索，我會學習某一領域的內容，但我不一定要從事這個領域。我在決定是否要進入那個領域之前，會先探索機會，通過一定的調查，你會知道這個行業是不是你想參與的。這樣，你就可以決定下一步。在人生當中，能探索新鮮事物是很好的，也能更好的挖掘出你潛在的能量。

3. Should I learn more different programming language?
   我是否應該學習不同的電腦程序語言？

   There is no harm in learning more as it will only broaden your knowledge in any field you choose to learn about.
   學習是百利而無一害的，它只會擴展你的知識。

4. What is your view on the importance of studying business related subjects in our present society?
   請問你認為修讀商科課程在現今社會中是否重要？

   It depends on who you work for and what is your job nature. You can learn about management in many ways. Work experience will usually be more important. I would recommend that you always further yourself with study part-time but it takes determination and self-discipline.
   這取決於你為誰工作以及你的工作性質，你會有很多方式學到管理，工作經驗通常來講要更為重要。我建議你可在空閑時間兼讀學習商科，但這也取決於你的決心和個人的自控能力。

5. How do you resolve the difficulties in studying computer programming at University? As you said during our luncheon, you hated two subjects, namely the study of

electricity and computer programming. Did you mean that you are not good at computer programming and how do you resolve this problem? (I am not good at computer programming and I hope you can offer some advice).

請問你是怎樣解決學習電腦程序科時遇到的問題？根據梁博士你於聚餐時所說，大學時，您最討厭的就是電學跟電腦程序科。請問這是指你不擅長電腦程序科嗎？請問你是怎樣解決這個問題？（因為我並不是十分擅長電腦程序科，所以希望請教你一些解決辦法。）

You can always be good at something if you work extra hard on the subject. I did not like programming and I thought it was boring but I needed to be good at it for my PhD studies. That was not by a matter of choice, it was a necessity. So the only solution or advice I can give is I think we have to work twice as hard at something we are not good at. It is not a matter of liking it or not. I still do not think I like it but I trust that I am quite good at it now. So like me, you have to work hard at it.

只要夠努力就一定能在某些方面取得成績。我不喜歡電腦程序因為我覺得它很悶，但我必須為了我的博士學位學好和應用它，這不是可以選擇的事，而是必須做到的。結果就是我付出了兩倍的努力來學好它。這並不關乎你喜愛與否，我到現在也不覺得我喜歡，但我要學得很好，而且現在我相信我已經在這方面精通了，所以努力專注是很重要的。

6. Is there any specific knowledge which is more important than others? At the luncheon, you said that we must "learn

everything; and equip yourself to grab the next opportunity". Are there any specific knowledge/language/skills that are more important in the future work environment? At the moment, I want to learn what I am interested in and I shall learn what I need for my work in the future. Do you think this is feasible?

請問有甚麼知識特別重要？聚餐時，您曾指出"咩都學"，"要裝備自己才可以捉緊機會"。請問有甚麼知識/語言/技術對日後工作特別重要？我現在先按自己興趣學習，日後工作時才針對需要來學習，請問這個方法可行嗎？

This depends on your focus and what direction you want to go in your work. You will need general knowledge e.g. what is going on in our society, who is who in the industry. You will need specific knowledge e.g. engineering knowledge, negotiation skills, public speaking etc. You will also need language skills e.g. Mandarin, Cantonese, English. All of the above you will need in order to prepare yourself for where you want to work or what you will be working in. You can always keep your interests so enjoy your University life now. This is the best time of your life. You can also learn and gain knowledge by travelling. Go beyond Hong Kong and see the world. You will see what other countries do and you will learn from seeing. You should become a person with international perspectives, so don't be limited by just only being in Hong Kong.

這取決於你以後想怎樣發展。你需要常識，比如說行業的趨勢，行業裏的人脈等。你也需要專業知識，例如工程學，談判技巧，演講技巧等。你還需要語言能力，如普通話，廣東話，英語等。你要為你的工作做好準備，你也可以同時保持你自己的興趣。享受你現在的大學生活。這是你人生中最美好的時光。可以去旅遊，走出香港，去看看世界，你應該成為一名國際人而不僅僅局限於香港，這樣你可以看到其他的國家如何處事，可以從中學習，獲益良多。

7. How does one balance academic studies with one's social life?

   請問你如何在學業和社交中取得平衡？

   If you are successful in school, then you have a good social life. If you failed in school, no one will pity you in society. Schooling should be a priority in your life right now. You can always have a good social life when you can make it in your career.

   如果你學業有成，那你會有很好的社交生活。如果你學業失敗，沒有人會同情和憐憫你。學校教育是你現在生活的優先部份。如果你能在事業上成功，那你的社交生活也一定沒問題了。

8. Do you have any books to recommend as "suggested reading"?

   您有沒有好建議的書給我閱讀呢？

   Any books that interest you can be "suggested reading". Books that are related to your profession may be of interest and should be read too e.g. books on negotiation, management, contract law, dispute resolution, advancement in technology, future trends, economics, public policies etc. 任何讓你覺得有趣的書都是好書，能與你本業有關的也是好的。有些參考書如談判技巧、管理學、合同法、糾紛處理、科技發展、未來趨勢、經濟學、公共政策等……

9. Many said that in construction industry, experience is more important than learning in school. It does not help one to find a job even after studying a master's degree. Some of my seniors have indicated that after they completed their master's, the larger companies do not value it much and

they want to change jobs because of this. What is your view?

聽人話建築行業經驗重要過學歷，其實讀完碩士後對搵工幫助大唔大？好似有師兄讀完後，公司都有乜表示，都想轉份工，您又點睇？

I agree that experience is vital in construction. Schooling will assist you to understand some of the basic technical issues in construction. I do not believe that a master's degree will help you to find job. It is your experience that helps more. A master's only certifies that you are academically qualified and it has nothing to do with finding job. It is the work experience that will help you. Your willingness and attitude towards work is also vital in getting a job and your experience will let you excel in your work. Most companies do not need a Master in Construction to work in construction. The master's will only help if you want to be an Academic. That is why some companies do not consider it any additional value for the company. Changing jobs may not improve the situation unless the new job provides more experience to the individual.

我同意經驗在建築行業很重要，學術理論可以輔助你去理解行業中的一些基本技術問題。我不覺得一個大學碩士學位就一定能幫助你找到工作，往往是經驗會幫助更多。碩士學位只是讓你在理論基礎方面有一定的資格認可，這對找工作意義並不是很大，而工作經驗是實實在在可以幫到你的。你努力做工的意向是找工作的重要因素之一。你的工作經驗可以幫助到你在公司中迅速增長。如果你想做一名學者或教書，碩士學位是能幫到你的。很多建築公司甚至是不需要碩士學位的，因為一個有碩士學位的人並不會為公司帶來更多大的優勢。更換一份工作不一定能改變這情況，除非新的工作可以提供更多的工作經驗給你。

10. There are many University students who have committed suicide due to pressure from their studies. Is there a problem with our education system?

前排有好多大學生因學習壓力太大，好多人都跳樓自殺，係唔係教育體制出現咗問題？

Accepting pressure or stress is part of life. Everyone needs to accept stress, especially in the construction industry. We are always under time and cost pressure and stress in construction works. One needs to know how to release stress at work or in school. One shall not take pressure or stress home. At times, there is so much pressure imposed by parents. Many parents want their children to get ahead in school and forget that the child needs to be treated as a child. I think problems often begin at home and parents must play their role to help their child. There is pressure in school but there is even greater stress from work. The child needs to learn how to accept stress as well as how to release stress. That is more fundamental.

能接受壓力是人生的一部分，每個人都需要接受壓力，特別是在建築行業，建築行業永遠有時間和成本的壓力。一個人需要知道如何在工作或學校裏釋放壓力，不應該把壓力帶回家。有很多父母對孩子施加壓力，他們希望自己的孩子在學校裏很優秀，卻忘記了他還是一個小孩子，要用正確的方式來教導他。很多時候，問題出自家庭教育，父母必須要做好自己的角色來幫助孩子學習如何接受壓力，如何釋放壓力，這才是治根的辦法。在學校裏有壓力，但在工作上壓力更大。

11. Do you think studying is the best way to get out of poverty?
    你認為讀書是否最有效的脫貧方法呢？

    Definitely. If you study and learn, you can improve yourself with knowledge and this is the means to earn more money in life. After graduating, you will have secured a certain standard of living and you will have a head start and excel faster than anyone who did not study at all.
    絕對是的，如果你願意讀書學習，你可以提高自己的知識水平，這意味着可能賺得更多。畢業後，你會有一定的基本生活保障水平，這樣你已勝在起點，也可以比那些不願意學習的人增長得更快。

12. Do you think there are problems with the education system in Hong Kong? They only seem to know how to spoon-feed materials to the students and grades are the determiner to successes in school.
    你認為香港的教育制度是否有問題？都是填鴨式和以考試為主導的學習模式。

    There are many things that we need to learn in life and there is often never enough time to do so. You will be under pressure in school as well as in life while working. You have to learn how to relieve your stress and learn how to relax. This is part of life. The education system in Hong Kong has room for improvement yet it has also created many great leaders in our community. There is always room for improvement in any system but we cannot change it in one day, so we just have to live with it. It is up to you to learn how to cope with it. It will be the same when you work. Just like how you have to learn how to accept the pressure come from your boss. I do not think you have much option in that situation. Therefore, learning how to relax is a life long art form that you need to learn in life.

人生有很多事情需要學習，而學習的時間往往並不足夠。不論在學校還是在工作中你都會有壓力，你要學習如何緩解壓力學會放鬆，這是人生的一部分。香港的教育制度是有改善的空間，但它同時也幫我們在體系內培養了很多優秀的人才和領袖。有改善的空間不代表我們明天就能夠完全改變，我們要學會如何適應現有制度。如何處理問題在於你自己，工作上一樣會有壓力的，你要學會如何接受老板給你的壓力，我不覺得你在這種情況有太多的選擇。學會放鬆是一門藝術，是你一生都需要學習的。

13. There's a saying, "one wins at the starting line". Do you agree and do you think a young person from lower income groups will find it even more difficult to succeed in our society?

對於一個人贏在起跑線上這個說法，你會不會認為出身基層的年輕人更難在社會上取得成功呢？

No, I believe Hong Kong provides many opportunities for anyone who is good at what they do. You can have a good start by having a University degree. It is not because of your background that your boss will value you. It is because of your ability to perform well that moves you up the ladder. No one has ever asked me who my parents are throughout my career. Most people do not know my background. Hong Kong does provide equal opportunities for anyone. It is you who determines your destiny and no one else.

不，我覺得香港為每個優秀的人才都提供機會。比如你有一個大學學位，這是一個好的開始，但你的老板並不會因為你的背景來判斷你的價值，而是看你所展示的能力使你有晉升的機會。我工作一輩子也沒有人問我父母是誰，他們多數不知道我的背景，全是靠你自己的能力決定你的未來。香港能為每一個人提供公平的競爭機會。

14. What is your view on the education system in China vs. Hong Kong?
你對中國和香港的教育有什麼看法？

Education only provides you with the basic knowledge, regardless of where you are trained. It does not provide you with all the knowledge in life. Neither system will teach you social skills etc. It is up to your own initiatives to go further in learning. I am sure there are pros and cons in both systems but I would trust myself more in learning rather than relying on any systems. Different countries have their own systems e.g. US vs. UK, UK vs. Australia, China vs. Hong

Kong. They still do not teach you everything. I learnt about construction after graduating from University. So at the end of the day, it is you who determines your own destiny, not the system.

不管你在哪裏學習，教育只能提供一些基本的知識，它不會為你提供生活上的一切知識，更不會教你任何社交技巧，這些是需要自己主動學習的。我相信，每個教育系統都有其優缺點。但我更相信自主學習能力，而不是依賴於任何系統。不同的國家有不同的系統例如美國和英國，英國和澳大利亞，中國和香港，不會有任何系統可以教會你一切。我也是在土木工程大學畢業後，才去學會如何做建築這一行的，所以歸根結底，是自己決定自己的命運。

15. Does it matter where one goes to school or to further education for one's future success?

在哪所學校讀書對你將來的成功有多大幫助？

Schooling helps you get to know some of the best friends you will have in your life. It teaches you the basics and shows you how to logically analyze problems in order for you to face problems in life. Some better schools will enable you in job-hunting so you have a better start than others. It will give you a better start at first but after you have some experience in work, which school you had attended won't matter anymore. Your experience will be worth much more. No one ever asked me which school I went to after my first job. In other words, it does not matter what you do, it is how good you are at what you do that matters. Working hard will bring you success in life.

在學校裏能讓你有機會結識到一些一生中最好的朋友，也能學到基本的知識，教你如何邏輯地分析問題，以便解決將來人生中的問題。有些好一些的學校也能讓你在找工作時比其他人有更好的起步點，但你有了工作經驗之後，畢業於哪一所學校並不是那麼重要了，工作經驗反而更為重要很多。我除了在第一份工作時，人事部了解我在哪裏畢業，以後便沒有人問我畢業於哪所學校了。從另一方面來看，做哪一行不重要，但做每一行都要做得最好才是最重要。勤奮工作更能讓你在人生中取得成功。

16. Does it matter what subjects one studied?

    決定學習哪一科究竟有多重要？

The subject you study will give you specific knowledge in the area but it does not mean that you will be working in the same field e.g. studied engineering and working in finance. As long as a student is prepared to learn continuously, he/she will excel in any area. There are no limits in learning. The day that you stop learning is the day you stop living and that's the day when you fail. You need to continue learning in order to be prepared for your next challenge.

選科會讓你了解到某個領域相關的知識，但這並不是說你以後一定會從事這個行業，比如你可讀工程但做財經。只要你願意持續學習，你在任何一個領域裏都有可能成功。學習是沒有止境的，當你停止學習的時候，才是你失敗的開始，你要學習才能為下一個挑戰作好準備。

17. Recently, there are more and more parents thinking of sending their children to study at international schools rather than local schools. Apparently, the community is dissatisfied with the local education system. What are your views? Can the current local education system lead the new generation to become more competitive? What changes should occur, if any?

近年來，有越來越多家長想送他們的孩子去國際學校讀書而不是本地學校。很顯然，公眾對於本地教育的爭論越來越多，你覺得本地教育怎樣？目前的本地教育可以引領新一代使他們更有競爭力嗎？有什麼需要改善的地方？

There are advantages in both types of school systems. At international schools, one may be able to benefit and learn more on languages, with exposure to different approaches in teaching and learning styles with smaller class sizes. However, there may be limited study and teachings on local history and information about our own country. In the local schools, one may learn more on technical subjects e.g. science and technology. Surely, every education system needs continuous improvement in order to catch up with the ever-changing society. So we need

NĬ Hǎo!
你好!
GOODBYE!

to train students to be prepared and ready for what's to come in life.

I think some students will learn more in different types of school. Some may do better in local schools than international schools. I wanted my daughter to learn Mandarin and English many years ago and that is why I sent her to an international school. In those days, local schools did not have Mandarin as a compulsory subject but this situation has changed since. The trade off was that Sciences were not my daughter's strength as she acquired better language skills as a result. This is just one real case example I can share.

So, I think it is important for the next generation to learn more about China. It is most probable that the future generations will need to work in both Hong Kong and China. They will need to learn and understand our history, our culture, and what the Chinese have done in the last 20 years. This will guide and prepare them for the challenges of tomorrow. I trust that our education system will need to consider and include this area of knowledge in schools. If the school system does not provide this, parents shall have to teach their child on their own to prepare them for the needs of tomorrow. One does not learn everything from schooling anyway; and as parents we want the best for our children and it is our responsibility to prepare them to face the challenges regardless of what school system they are in.

兩種學校都有他們的優勢。在國際學校，可以學到更多的語言，每班的人數較少，教學的方式不同，但很少學習到我們自己國家的知識。在本地學校，學生可以學到多一些理科方面的教育，如科學與科技等。當然每一個教育體系都需要持續不斷的進步才能跟上時代，我們要訓練孩子們為明天做好準備。我覺得學生在不同形式的學校可以學到不同的東西，有些可能會在本地學校好過國際學校。很多年前，我希望我的女兒學普通話和英文，當時很多本地學校根本沒有普通話學習，因此我送她去國際學校讀書，但這樣她的理科就不如她的語言科目那麼好。這只是其中一個案例，我覺得對於年輕一代來講，很重要的一點是他們要學習和明白我們的祖國，因為他們在未來很有可能要在中國國內和香港工作，他們要學習並且知道自己的歷史、文化以及中國過去二十年的努力，這樣會引導他們走向未來。我相信我們的教育系統需要增加這方面的學習機會。如果學校的系統沒有提供，家長也要自行教育自己的孩子，學校不可能教會你孩子所需的一切，作為家長總是希望為孩子提供最好的，不論那一個學校的系統有否提供，我們作為家長都有責任裝備好孩子，來面對未來的挑戰。

18. In one's early days of his/her career, what do I need to learn about?

在我剛出道時，我需要學習到什麼？

You will need to learn about China, learn about its history and what China went through in the past years. China's stable economy and political stability did not come easy. China has been through many wars and the Chinese people have suffered as a consequence. We as Chinese people do not want to experience war and civil turmoil again. In fact, it's most regretful that Chinese history is no longer a compulsory subject in high school. That is because before we can start to create and build a better future, we have to understand what went on in the past. I personally have spent time living abroad and understand that if China is not a strong, powerful nation, Chinese people will be always be disrespected. So as a Chinese, we must prove and demonstrate our strength to the rest of the world; and be able to stand on our own two feet. We cannot rely on other countries to create our own prosperity, no matter who rules China.

你需要學習中國，學習它的歷史，知道中國以前經歷過什麼。如今中國穩定的經濟發展和政治體制得來並不容易，中國曾經多年處於戰亂，人民飽受戰亂的痛苦，作為中國人我們不會願意再次經歷戰爭和動亂。中國歷史科沒有作為高中的必修課，其實很是遺憾，我們在創造未來之前應該先了解過去。我本人曾經在海外多年，很清楚如果中國不強大，別人不會尊重你。作為中國人，我們必須向世界證明和展示自己的實力，而且需要自力更生。不管中國的當權者是誰，我們都不能依靠別的國家來建造本國的繁榮。

19. If I want to become more knowledgeable, intellectual and smart, what kind of books should I read?
有什麼書可以讓我獲得更多的知識並且變得更聰明呢？

All books will give value to you in life because you do not

know when it will come in handy. I have read different materials at different stages of my life. I try to read books, texts, materials that will assist me in my work as well as for pleasure e.g. I read a lot on arbitration, mediation, engineering, real estate, construction, law, optical fiber, as well as journals, fiction and non-fiction books. I will read anything that comes across my path.

任何書都有它的價值,因為不知何時可以用得着。我在不同的時段看很多不同的書,我會看一些參考書幫助我的工作和休閒閱讀,例如我會看有關仲裁、調解、工程、房地產、建築、法律、光纖、專業學會期刊、小說和現實故事等等,所有有趣的書我都會看。

20. In what ways can I train myself to be a smarter person?
我怎樣可以把自己訓練成一個聰明人？

I don't consider myself as a smart person, yet I don't think I am stupid either, so I still need to continuously learn new things and gain more knowledge. I do not think you can be truly smart unless you are extremely knowledgeable in a variety of areas. Being smart, or not, is relative. One should not compare oneself with others. Just do the best that you can in life and never believe that you are a smart person. There will always be someone out there who is smarter than you.

我覺得我自己不算是一個聰明人但也不笨，所以我還需要學習。我不覺得你會成為一名聰明的人，聰明與否是相對的。不要拿你自己和別人比較，只要你自己在人生中做到最好。也不要相信自己是一個聰明人，永遠有人是比你更聰明的。

21. What is the most important quality a great leader must possess?
一個優秀的領導者要具備哪些重要的因素？

A great leader should be able to share knowledge. That is what makes people respect you. A great leader always

點

解

teaches skills and shares experience with others. A great leader will create better leaders of tomorrow. A leader is someone who you respect and look up to. I hope all my students will be better than me in the future and then I know I have become a great leader.

分享知識是一個優秀的領導者應該做的事，這才是他人尊重他的原因。做一個好的領導者要把他的技能和經驗傳授給別人，也要為將來培育更好的領導者。我希望你將來會比我更好，這樣我才能成為一名優秀的領導者。一名領導者應該是你尊敬並且景仰的人。

22. What books should I read and what habits should I form that will make me improve and become successful in life?

有哪些書和習慣可以使我提升自己並且成為一位成功者？

I read all kinds of books since I do not know when it will come in handy for future use. You can read books on administration and management to behavioral and skills development but many of these books only focus on the theory. You will need to find books that are practical and applicable to your needs. I trust all books will give some inspiration in life. However, you may not realize it at the time of reading. This is known as unconscious learning. So the more you learn, the more you will improve on the quality of life. The meaning of success is different for each person and one should never compare oneself with others. If you have tried hard and done your best, you will always be the best.

我看很多不同類型的書，因為我不知道我何時會需要用到。

你可以讀一些關於行政管理和技能提升的書，但有很多書都過於理論化，你要找一些可以在實踐中用得着的書。我相信所有的書都可以在我人生中帶來亮點，可能我看的時候並不一定意識到這一點。你讀的書越多，越能無形地改善到你的人生。成功是相對的，每個人成功的定義都不同，你不應該和他人比較，只要你盡了最大的努力，你就是最好的。

23. How does academic study affect your career?
   學術研究對你的工作有何影響？

I did both of my Master and PhD degrees on a part-time basis and I took many other courses on a part-time basis too throughout my career. It did not affect my career at all. To me, I felt that I needed to learn more in order to improve. Academic studies will help you to think logically but it is not the only thing you need. One needs to balance reality with theory. There are many things that one needs to learn and I believe that study and continuous learning is the only way that one can keep up with the times and our ever-changing society.

我利用公餘的時間兼讀完成了我的碩士和博士學位，這是完全沒有影響到我的工作，我認為我需要不斷學習來改進自己。學術研究幫助你理性思考，但這並不是一切，每個人也需要學會平衡現實與理論。這世界實在有太多知識需要學習了，我覺得學習是唯一能讓一個人進步和與時並進的方法。

24. I am not a nervous person, but I can't seem to present myself very clearly in front of a group of people. How can I improve my presentation skills?

點
解

我要怎樣可以提高我的演講技巧？我並不是緊張，而是在很多人面前就很難清晰地表達自己。

It takes practices. It takes a lot of practice! You need to build your confidence by knowing the subject well. You need to be well prepared. You need to learn the appropriate body language to attract your audience. Maintaining eye contact is also very important as well as your tone of voice. Prepare, prepare, and prepare. Practice, practice, and practice. As you do it more frequently, you will improve and get better.

這是需要練習的。你首先要深入了解和認識你要講的題目，來建立好自己的自信心，要做好準備功夫。你還需要一定的肢體語言來吸引你的聽眾，眼神接觸交流是非常重要的。做好準備，再次準備。練習，再次練習，只要多練習，你一定可以越來越好的。

25. How can I be confident if I have not succeeded in anything yet?

如果我在任何方面都不優秀，我要怎樣才能有自信呢？

You are a graduate student, which means you are already more successful than many others in our society. As a graduate student, you have attained a certain level of knowledge. Do not underestimate your own ability. You are better than you think. With knowledge and hard work you will gain more self-confidence and be able to reach new heights.

你是一名研究生，已經比我們社會中的許多人成功，你已經達到一定的知識水平，才能成為研究生。不要低估自己的能力。你比你所想像的更好。有了知識和努力工作，你將獲得更多的自信，達到新的領域。

點
解

26. Two years ago, I never thought of getting a master's degree and now, having spent a lot of money, time and effort, I am working hard to achieve it. I know that in order to further develop myself, when I graduate, I will consider a PhD or another master's degree in another field or even study a degree in Law or Civil Engineering. So I was wondering, is environmental law popular in Hong Kong? If I was to get a bachelor's degree in Law, in addition to my knowledge in environmental sciences, is that enough to become an environmental lawyer?

兩年前我還不認為自己可以獲得環境碩士學位的，但到現在我花了很多錢也付出了很多努力來爭取這個學位。我知道當我畢業後，我會問自己是否要再讀博士或者是其它專業的學位，如法律或土木工程科，以便讓我自己更進一步。在香港作為一名環境科律師普遍嗎？如果我有法律學士，再加上我在環境科的認識，這樣我是否足夠能做一個環境科律師呢？

Never underestimate yourself if you are determined to do something. It can be hard work but one day it will pay off. Obtaining a PhD is for one whose interest is to teach or do research in a specialised field. It may not be too useful for a person working in the industry. If you want to teach and do research in the future, then it will be a good choice. However, work experience is more important in any industry. You can consider doing another master's degree or study Law. Presently, there are not too many environmental lawyers in Hong Kong and as environmental issues are becoming more and more important in Hong Kong, I am sure there will be lots of interesting developments ahead. If you study Law along with practical work experience in the field of environmental science, I am sure this will help you become a good environmental lawyer.

如果你下定決心去做一件事情，就不要低估自己的能力。可能會有一段日子很難熬但總有一天會有收獲的。博士學科是為了那些有興趣做教育或者研究工作的人，可能對你在社會上工作便不是很有用。如果你想要教書或者做研究，那這是一個很好的方向。在行業裏，工作經歷反而更重要。你也可以考慮法律學士，現在香港的環境科律師並不多，但環境問題越來越嚴重，我想這也可能會是一個很有意思的方向。如果你學了法律並有環境方面的實踐工作經驗，這當然會幫助你成為一個好的環境科律師，祝你好運。

27. What are my strengths and what am I really good at?

怎樣可以知道我自己的實力，我擅長於什麼呢？

You can be good at anything if you continuously work on a particular issue. When you have tried your hardest, you are at your best and it will become your strength. It is not a matter of whether you like it or not, but if keep working hard, it will bring out your strengths in life.

只要你持續不斷地去做某一事情，你一定會做得很好。當你盡到自己最大的努力，你就會達到高峰，而這也就是你的實力，不論你喜不喜歡這個事情，只要你不斷努力工作，便會將你的能量發揮出來的。

28. What will you achieve as a Mentor under this mentorship program?

作為一個導師，你在導師/學員計劃中有何得着？

I enjoy and want to help young people. I believe that many of our younger generation need guidance. For me, I wish I had the opportunity to join a mentorship program when I was young. So I want to share my knowledge, as I know it will assist others to excel. To be able to share and give my honest opinion is my only goal and it is up to the Mentees to accept it or not. Sharing with others is happiness in one's life.

我喜歡也希望幫助年輕人，因為我認為很多年輕人需要指引。如果我以前也能有導師學員計劃的機會就好了。我想分享我的經驗給他人，使他人有所得着。我只能提供我最真誠的意見，學員要自己決定接受與否。分享本身已是人生快樂的一部份。

29. What do you expect from your Mentees?

你希望你的學員是怎樣的？

Actually, I have no expectations from my Mentees. As long as one wants to learn, one must show self-initiative. It is up to the individual to determine how much assistance he or she requires and to take the initiative for him or herself. My role is to be here and teach, guide and assist all my Mentees.

我對我的學員沒有任何要求，一個人想學習，他一定要有自我學習的主動性。事實上，是學員自己決定他/她需要多少幫助和指引，我只是在輔助、教導和協助我的學生。

30. Why and for what reason was I selected as a Mentee?
    是哪一點吸引你通過我的申請考核？

I believe all of the Mentee applications are young people with initiative to improve. You all showed a willingness to learn from an experienced Mentor and this modest desire or "hunger" to learn will ultimately lead you onto a new and unexpected life path.

我認為所有學員都是自主地希望提升自己的，同時每一位也希望和樂意向較有經驗的導師學習。"求知若渴，虛心若愚"會帶你去到一個意想不到的新目標。

31. How does one stop wasting time?
    怎樣可以停止浪費時間？

Simply pick up a book. Refrain from playing video games or watching TV is my advice. I recall when I was studying for my part-time PhD or while I was writing books, the best advice given to me was that I had to choose between watching TV or going to work on my computer. Sometimes this can be a difficult decision to make in one's life. Learn to observe others' behavior, learn from your surroundings, and do things that are constructive to your life.

拿起一本書，停止玩遊戲機或者看電視。當我兼讀我的博士學位和寫書時，我便要在看電視和用電腦工作之間作出選

點
解

擇，要玩樂還是要工作，決定確實不容易。要學會觀察別人的行為，從你周圍的事物中學習，更重要是做一些有建設性的事情。

32. How does one differentiate between what is right and what seems to be right?

如何區分出什麼是對的，而什麼是看上去正確但事實上只是他人的想法。

With sufficient knowledge and logical analysis, you can determine what is right. If it seems to be right then it is not right and you should proceed with caution. What seems to be right for others may not be right for you. You have to determine what is right in life for yourself because you are the one who will have to live with the consequences and ultimately responsible for any wrong decisions you make. Therefore you need to logically analyze the situation with facts before you make your final decision.

你要利用你的學識和邏輯分析能力來判斷什麼對與錯。如果只是看上去是對的，那它可能不對。你要特別小心來處理。有些看上去對他人是對的事情，但對你來說並不一定合適。你要為自己的人生做出正確的選擇，因為你最終要為你作出的錯誤決定負上責任。所以你需要理性地分析事情，才能作出最後的決定。

33. If you were 20 to 25 year old again, what kind of work would you do? (not a part-time job or summer intern job)

如果你還是20-25歲，你會做什麼（不僅是兼職或暑期工）？

I would find a summer job. I would study hard. I would participate in sports. I would enjoy my University life. I would try to get the grades that will enable me to get into graduate school, should I decide to go to graduate level. The truth is, after gradating I went to find work right away and completed my Masters by studying part-time.

我會做暑期工，努力讀書，參加各項運動，享受我的大學生活。如我想讀碩士課程，我會盡量獲得足夠畢業的學分使我能再繼續進修。在現實中，我畢業工作後，利用兼讀完成了我的碩士課程。

34. What should I do as a pre final year student?
作為一個快要畢業的學生，我該做些什麼？

See the world. Enjoy your final year. This is the best time of your life. Establish friendships, as these may be your lifelong friends. Be prepared for new challenges. Be prepared for downtime, frustrations and depression, as this is also part of life. One needs to learn how to accept and move on to reach the next milestone.

去看一看世界，享受你大學最後的一年，這是你一生最美好的時光。結交朋友，這些可能是你一生受用的朋友。為新的挑戰做好準備，也為沮喪做好準備並坦然接受，這是人生的一部分。有些人需要學習怎樣接受和如何向前翻開新的里程碑。

35. How was your University life at the University of Toronto?
    你在多倫多大學時的大學生活是怎樣的？

It was truly enjoyable, lots of hard work, and I experienced many ups and downs. I enjoyed my time at University so much that I almost failed in my first year, and then I began to realize that I needed to study. Therefore, I improved in my grades from second year onwards and finally graduated with honors. That's how I got into the part-time graduate program. I enjoyed the days that I spent at Robarts Library and the nights spent in the computer room trying to get the assignments done; and the conception of the Chinese Engineering Student Association, the many parties we had, and of course eating many dinners at New College. So my University life was fun and colourful filled with many wonderful and unforgettable days.

當年非常愉快，努力學習，有起有落。我太喜歡校園生活以至於在第一年考試差一點過不了關，那時我才意識到我需要努力讀書。所以第二年開始，我努力學習，並且最終在畢業時得到榮譽學位，這樣我才能以兼讀方式去讀我的碩士學位。我懷念曾在Robarts圖書館的日子，夜晚在電腦室為了完成電腦作業而努力的日子，中國工程學生會的組成和聚會，在New College的晚餐，我相信我的大學生活是多姿多彩的，也有很多非常難忘的日子。

36. As an Environmental Engineering graduate, I couldn't agree more with your perspective on life – life is always changing. Three years ago, I couldn't even imagine myself in the construction industry, but life took me on a strange ride along with some confusion and anxiety. Before, I used to think engineering was a very strange field yet having worked in this industry; I decided to take the HKUST's Master of Environmental Engineering program to learn more about engineering. Having now been in the workforce for a year and half, I began to realize that there is a need for a different type of professional qualification or membership, and a master's degree alone is not enough. My first question is, what kind of membership will best suit me? The Hong Kong Institute of Engineers (HKIE) membership is one of the most common in the industry and they also have environmental related divisions. The problem is that I don't have a bachelor's degree in Engineering and I don't know if they will accept my master's degree in Environmental Engineering as an equivalent. My second question is, do you have any students in the same situation? If so, could you share their experience?

作為一個環境工程學位的學生，我非常同意你對人生的觀點，人生總是不停地改變的。三年前，我甚至不能想像我自己會在建築行業，但人生卻帶我到了這個陌生的領域，當時我也曾感到混亂焦慮。我在這家公司工作之前，工程對我來說是一個非常陌生的領域，因此，我讀了科大的環境工程碩士課程，以了解更多關於環境工程的知識。現在，我在這裏工作了一年半，我開始意識到需要有不同的專業資格認證，僅靠碩士學位是不足夠的。我第一個問題是，哪個學會的會籍是最適合我目前的情況？我知道香港工程師學會是工程界別最常用的學會，他們也有環境學科。問題是，我沒有工程學士學位，我不知道他們是否會接受我工程碩士學位作為同等學歷。你有學生遇到同樣的情況？如果有，能否和我分享一下他的經驗？

I think you can first register with the HKIE's Environmental Division. At the HKIE, they have Civil, Building, Environmental, and IT divisions, just to name a few. Once you get the first qualification from HKIE, you can also join different disciplines at a later date so as to improve your knowledge e.g. I am three divisions - Civil, Building and IT. I joined them each at different stages of my career. There are various qualifications and requirements for each division i.e. work experience. One can join up to three disciplines without additional fees. Please consider this and make your enquiries with HKIE. Please contact them directly for the requirements. I think a master degree will be sufficient as some environmental science graduates also joined the Civil division, so it is largely depends on your work experience.

我覺得你可以先在香港工程師學會環境學科註冊，在香港工程師學會，他們有土木工程、大樓建築、環境、電信小組等，一旦你在學會獲得了首個認可資格，你就可以加入不同的小組，增加知識。例如，我參加了土木工程、大樓建築、

電信小組，我在人生的不同時段加入到這些不同的小組，每
組都有不同的資格要求，如工作經驗和學歷要求，每個工程
師可以免費加入三個不同的小組。你可考慮一下並且和他們
直接咨詢一下，我認為碩士學位是夠資格的。有些環境科學
生也加入到土木工程小組的，這更取決於你的工作經驗。

37. How is the standard of Hong Kong construction comparable
with the Mainland China? For example, in the self-climbing
formwork trade, it seems widely used in Mainland China yet
we seldom use this in Hong Kong. Is Hong Kong lagging
behind?
其實香港嘅建築水平同大陸比較係點樣？好似自動爬升板模
係香港用得好少，但係聽人話大陸已經運用得好成熟，係唔
係香港落後咗？

There are major differences between Hong Kong and
Mainland China. In China, their construction units are mostly
labor contractors. The Project Management office will do
all the acquisition and coordinate all the works. The Main
Contractor is usually a labor contractor only. In the past 10
years, China has advanced more than Hong Kong in the
construction industry in some respects. This is because they
have huge engineering projects that can take advantage
of the latest technology in the industry. However, I think
Hong Kong is still leading in terms of contract, electrical
and mechanical construction, coordination of works, fitting
out works, design, and sales and marketing strategies. We
cannot say that who is ahead in the industry since there

is still much to be learned. We need to learn not only from China but also from the rest of the world in order for our industry to move forward, and we must keep an open mind and attitude towards learning from others.

香港和中國有很大區別，在中國國內，他們的施工單位主要是勞動承包商，業主代表辦公室做所有的采購和協調施工的工作，總承包商主要為勞動力和土建承包商。在過去的十多年裏，中國在有些方面比香港的建築行業更超前。因為他們有巨大的工程項目，可以運用行業中的最新技術。然而，講到合同方面、機電施工、協調工作、裝修工程、設計、銷售策略等，我認為香港仍然處於行業中的領先地位。我們不能說誰是處於行業領先地位，因為有很多地方還需學習。日日新鮮，這也是為什麼我們要向全世界各地學習，不僅是中國，這樣香港才可以更向前走一大步。當我們學習時，我們必須保持一個開放的態度。

38. When there are many requisite time periods for different scenarios, for example what is the required number of days to give notice for a certain situation, what is a good method for remembering them all?

一個課題裏有很多指定日子需要記得，比如有一些特定日子要事先通知業主的要求，有什麼好的記憶方法使我記得這些日子？

If you understand the basic principles of the subject, you can divide it up by way of using a matrix chart to help you remember. Giving notice is always needed in making claims so it is a matter of figuring out what type of contract is being

135

used and the variations in different contracts should only have minor differences to the number of days required.

如果你理解到主題的基本原則，你可以用表格方式來區分不同的情況，相信這會幫助你記得需要的日子。在很多合同中，申請追索條款中通常都需要一定的預先通知期限，只是不同的合同對所需的天數稍有差別而已。

My Sharing
我的分享

Learning can bring opportunities. One learns to improve cognition. One learns to create new ideas. One learns to apply what you learnt. Different subjects can be learnt depending on what your own interests and where you work. You should be flexible in your learning. You should have an open mind and attitude since you will not know when you will use what you have learnt. You can learn different skills to assist your work. The needs in your life will dictate what you need to learn. It is not a matter of liking the subject or not. It is a necessity in life.

學習可以帶給你機會，每個人都可以通過學習提升思考能力，創造新的思維，同時還要相結合學習與實踐，不同方面的學習取決於你自己的興趣和工作。學習是需要靈活的，要秉承開放的態度，因為你不知道什麼時候能用得上你所學到的東西。你可以學習不同的技能來提升你的工作效率，人生的各種機遇會決定你需要學習哪些技能，這與喜好無關，而是生活中必須掌握的。

You can balance your learning with your social life. You can also learn through your social life. You can learn from anyone and you should make use of the opportunity to learn. Both academic studies and life experiences are important in anyone's life. One can provide you with a better start in life and other will make you excel in ways you never thought could be possible. Different education systems will provide you with different experiences. One should always treasure these experiences. One should treasure the years of study and the friends made during this period of life. They will likely become your lifelong friends.

你完全可以平衡學習與你的社交活動，當然，你也可以通過你的社交活動來學習人生，從每一個人身上學習到知識，要好好把握每個學習的機會。 學歷和工作經驗在人生中都很重要，學歷可以幫你有一個更好的起點，工作經驗使你快速成長。不同的教育制度也會使你得到不同的經驗，要好好珍惜這些經驗。要珍惜你的學生時代和你在這期間中所遇到的朋友，他們會是你人生中的長期夥伴。

Lastly, I think it is important for one to appreciate what can be achieved through learning as well as realising what you intend to achieve in your life. If you do not know something, you can always learn to find the answer and excel. If face different obstacles in life, you can overcome them by learning new things. Never underestimate yourself and you will be surprised with what you can achieve in life, especially when you put your heart into learning.

最後，一個人要懂得分辨哪些是通過學習可以獲取，哪些是你有打算將來想要達成的。如果有什麼不懂的，可以通過學習來找到答案。你可以通過學習新的事物來克服人生中的不同障礙，一定不要低估自己的能力，只要你用心學習，你會得到更多驚喜的收穫。

Work
工作

Work is part of everyone's life and having a job or career is an essential aspect of one's life. It provides us with satisfaction and reward that can fulfill our needs in life. It motivates one to work harder. It can also bring stress to one's life. One needs to maintain a good balance and harmony between work and stress in order to have a fruitful and fulfilling career.

工作是人生中很關鍵的部分，它可以為我們提供生活所需，可以激勵我們更加努力地工作，但同時也會給個人帶來一定的壓力。要平衡工作和壓力之間的和諧，才會有一個更有意義和令你滿意的職業生涯。

We all need to learn how to behave in the work environment; like how to work and deal with others, how to maximise our productivity, how to gain trust in others, how to find job satisfaction etc. Young people are often anxious about their first job or worry about changing jobs. They may consider self-employment vs working for others. These are all important decisions. One must address these questions in a positive and pro-active manner. I trust this chapter will provide some of the answers.

我們需要學習：如何在工作上與他人相處，在工作上的規矩，如何增加自己的生產力，怎樣獲得他人的信任，怎樣在工作中取得成就感等等。年輕人有時會關注他們選擇的第一份工作或擔心轉換工作，他們還會對創業或打工作出比較，這些問題都是他們一生中的重要決定，必須積極主動地去解決這些問題。我希望這章能為你提供一些答案。

Questions & Answers:

問題和答案:

1. What should I do if I am working in a company where my co-workers treat me badly and leaving the company is not an option?

   如果我在一家公司其他人對我很不友好，而我又不能離開，我該怎麼辦？

   Control your emotions. Accept other people and their views. Review and assess why they treat you badly; and think about what you can do to improve and achieve what is required of you. Are others correct in their way of working? Sometimes, silence can be the best option until you have the opportunity to move on.

   控制你的情緒，接受他人及其意見，回想為什麼別人對你不友好，你有什麼可以改進的地方，他們的工作方式是否正確，在你有其他選擇之前，保持沉默是最佳選擇。

2. How do you balance between work and family?

   你如何平衡工作與家庭？

   I try to spend as much time with my family as possible. Your family is your sanctuary and they are the only ones who you can rely upon when in need. They will not harm you in any way. That is what family is all about. They are the most trustworthy people you can count on. Family is where you can relax and be yourself. Work is also important. So you need to spend time on it in order to progress and excel.

You need to be committed and earn the trust from your boss. You need to achieve and perform accordingly and as to what is required of you from your boss. There will be situations where you need to make certain life choices and throughout the stages of life, one must start by working hard to set up a strong foothold for life.

我會盡量與我的家人花費最多的時間。家庭是你的庇護所，他們也是你在需要的時候能夠依賴和信任的，家人永遠不會傷害你，家庭是你休息放鬆和做回自己的地方。工作很重要，你必須要花很多時間才能進步，才會變得優秀。你必須要努力獲得老板的信任。在你的人生階段，有時會有需要你選擇的情況出現，我覺得你要更努力工作才能為你的人生打下好的基礎。

3. Doing the same job day by day has made me lose my passion for work and life. How can my job be interesting and inspiring again?

每天做同樣的工作，讓我對生活和工作都失去了熱衷，我應該怎樣做才可以找回工作的興趣？

You can learn from your job on a daily basis. You learn from the people around you. You learn from your boss and

143

you can learn from external sources other than your job. You should observe what others do in your surroundings. Your job is the basis for you to earn a living; yet it does not provide you with all the knowledge. Go to seminars or join an interest group. See the world and learn from others.

你要在每天的工作中學習，向你周圍的人學習，向你老板學習，你要觀察周圍的人在做什麼，你從這些資源上學到的遠多於你的工作本身。你的工作只是你生存的基礎，並不會真正教到你全面的知識，去研討會，去看看世界來學習他人。

4. How can we do the things we want to do?

   我们要怎樣做到自己想做的事？

   Just do it. Nothing is stopping you from doing something that you like. You have to like it very much to commit to it. Talk is useless. One needs to put things into action and complete tasks at hand. Accomplishment only comes from completed tasks. One can dream and speak in vain but if you do not complete the tasks involved, you will never succeed.

   盡管去做就是了，沒有什麼可以阻止你做自己喜歡的事情。你必須要非常喜歡才會願意全身心投入，空談理想是沒有用的，任何事情需要付諸行動並且努力完成。每個人都可以有夢想，但只有完成挑戰，才會成功。

5. How does one manage a difficult situation at work?

   你是如何處理工作上的困境？

點
解

Your boss will always know better than you. That is why he is your boss. Be open-minded and seek for solutions. If you cannot help your boss, he does not need you. Remember that you work for your boss. He does not work for you. There is an old saying, "The Boss is always right". You cannot be the problem for your boss. You have to learn to resolve problems.

老板一定比你知道得更多，這也是為什麼他是你的老板。現實地說，如果你無法幫助他，他也就不需要你了。不要忘記你是為他工作，不是他為你工作。有句老話說"老板永遠是對的"，你要幫他解決問題，而不是為他製造問題。

6. How can one manage time better and maximise on efficiency at work?

怎樣可以有效地管理好你的時間並讓工作效益最大？

Focus on a single issue or task at any one time. Complete one task before moving onto another. You can only work on a single issue or task at any given time. Try to complete your work today and do not wait till tomorrow. There are always new tasks for tomorrow. Try not to accumulate your work. Finish it today. Organise your work priorities and delegate your work if possible. Focus, focus and focus.

要集中所有注意力在一件事情上，完成一項工作才進行另一項，一次只能做一件事。盡量在當天完成工作而不要等到明天，因為明天永遠有新的工作。盡量不要累積工作，今日事今日畢！管理好工作的優先順序，一定要專注，專注，再專注！

7. How does one adapt and adjust to a new working environment? According to what you said in our lunch meeting, you have worked in a number of different companies and each time you changed jobs, there were some issues you encountered e.g. hidden customs within the company culture or groups of individuals in different factions. These are not stated clearly in any documentation but will affect future work relationships. How do you deal with these situations?

請問你是怎樣適應新的工作環境？按你聚餐時所說，您曾經在多間公司工作過，每當轉換新的工作時，都有很多需要適應的地方，例如一些潛在規則、黨派等，這些都不會白紙黑紙地向新人說明，卻會影響我以後在工作上的關係，請問你是怎樣去適應這些問題？

Every company has its own set of rules and style of management e.g. one boss may yell at you, another does not. You need to know what makes your boss yell at you. Others may want you to consult him on every detail, while others may not. You will need to be aware of the circumstances. Be on the look-out and be on your toes. Be alert and aware of your surroundings. Pay attention to your co-workers and observe how they handle others. One boss may yell at you all the time yet he means no harm, except for the fact that he does not want you to repeat the same mistake again, and so you can learn during the process. Be flexible and always be ready for change.

每個公司都有他們自己的規則和管理方式。例如，有一些老板會罵人，有些不會，你必須要知道為什麼他會罵你。有些老板可能會願意和你溝通每一個細節，有些可能不需要。你必須明白週邊的環境，隨時關注，留意你的同事如何處理事情。有些老板會罵你僅僅是因為他不想你再犯同一個錯誤，這樣你可以在過程中學習，學會靈活變通，並且隨時為改變做好準備。

8. How does one determine who is a good boss? This is a problem I faced in the past. I had two bosses. One had a strong personality and always yelled at his staff (and even the clients) but he was often right. The other boss was very

friendly and rarely yelled at his staff. Whenever the first boss was on duty, no one dared to be lazy but we experienced much grief. When the other boss was on duty, the work environment was friendlier but not as efficient as with the first boss. With two such diverse management styles, which is better? The high-pressure style or the friendlier style?

請問怎樣才是一名好的上司？這是一個我在過去工作上遇到的問題。當時我有兩位上司，一位十分兇，卻絕不是無理取鬧；另一位則十分友善，極少會責罵下屬。前者當值的時候，沒有任何人會敢偷懶，但招來不少怨氣（有時甚至在客人面前爆發出來）；另一位當值的時候，下屬雖不至於偷懶，卻明顯做得比平時慢，可是職場的氣氛卻十分和諧。對於這兩種相對的管理方法，我想問哪一種較好？是高壓政策還是懷柔政策？

A good boss is always willing to teach his staff. He will always try to help his staff to accomplish tasks. Different bosses have different styles. They all want you to do what they require of you. Their presentation skills may differ. On the contrary, some staff need to be yelled at before they will do their work, and some do not. Different types of people will receive different treatment. In reality, a boss needs to use different styles towards different types of people. Moreover, as a staff you need to tailor your style to suit your boss's style. At the end of the day, your boss/job requires you to complete your tasks so that work is being done. Some bosses may want to show off their superiority in front of others and you will need to accept this as his style.

Different styles match different people and under different circumstances.

一個好的老板會願意教他的員工，他會一直盡量幫助他的員工完成工作任務。不同的老板有不同的方式，他們希望你做他們想要你做的事情，他們所展示的態度可能不同。另一方面，有一些員工可能需要被罵才會去做他們的工作。事實上，一個老板需要用不同的工作方式來面對不同的員工。另外，作為一個員工，你也需要迎合你老板的工作方式，他們其實最終希望和需要的是你能完成你的工作。有一些人可能喜歡在其他人面前顯示他的權威，你也必須要明白並且接受。在不同的情況下，不同的人總是有不同的工作方式。

9. How can a fresh graduate, newly entering into the workforce fulfill the requirements of his boss or managers? Many reports say that young people often do whatever they want or they only know how to study. I agree with you completely in that a fresh graduate is a blank sheet of paper and the business world is a battlefield. University graduates are only equipped with a small knife upon graduation. When we try to use the knowledge learnt at school, we are often criticised on only knowing how to study. When we try to use our common sense, we are criticised for doing whatever we want. I understand it is difficult to satisfy my boss. At first, we have very little to offer. What can we rely on when on the job?

請問作為一個初入職場的大學生（尤其是工程相關的），應該怎樣滿足上司要求？很多新聞都指很多老闆不滿我們年輕人自把自為，死讀書等等。我十分同意您曾於聚餐中指出大

學生只是一張白紙，什麼都不懂。商場如戰場，我們大學生
只有從大學中得到的一把小刀，卻要面對槍林彈雨。當我們
打算靠大學的知識做事的時候，往往被批評為死讀書；當
我們捨棄大學知識，靠直覺做事的時候，卻被批評為自把自
為。我明白有時的確是我們無法滿足上司的要求，責無旁
貸，但我們什麼都沒有，到底我們應靠什麼做事呢？

I believe that completing the work assigned to you is the
most important purpose for hiring you. You are here to get
the work done. Most bosses have their own way of doing
things and it has been proven to work for them in the past.
Therefore, they may want you to follow their footsteps
because it has been proven to be successful already. They
do not want you to make mistakes because mistakes will
cost them. Studying only helps you to identify and analyse
the problem at hand. If your boss has the solutions, then
you can follow them to get the work done. If your boss
has no solutions, then you have to analyse the problem
and find solutions under the advice of your boss. Intuition
comes from knowledge. You have to use your logical mind
to analyse problems, which is what you learnt in school.
You can always suggest solutions and obtain your boss's
approval. Without consulting your superiors, should a
mistake arise, will be you who has to shoulder all the
consequences of acting on your own accord. You should
not act alone unless you are absolutely sure of the solution.
我相信完成工作任務是最重要的，很多老板都有他們自己做
事的方式而且這個方式是通過驗證的，因此他們希望你能夠

跟隨他們的步伐，他們不希望你犯錯因為這樣會增加成本。學習只能協助你找出解決問題的方式，如果你的老板已經有了解決辦法，你可以跟隨，如果他沒有解決辦法，你要分析問題，找出辦法請示他尋求意見。直覺是來自於知識，你可以先向他表達解決方法並獲取他的批準，如果你不提前和他溝通，一旦出現錯誤那將由你一個人承擔所有責任和後果。除非你非常確定答案，才能獨自行動，你要運用你的邏輯思維來分析問題，這也是大學所教導你的。

10. When I need to supervise a team and I encounter uncooperative team members, what technique can I use to ensure we achieve our objective and maintain good relations among team members?

請問當我需要管理一個團隊，而遇上團隊中的成員不合作的情況，有什麼技巧可以讓事情達致目標而又處理好團隊之間的關係？

Good working relationships and teamwork will make it easier for the team to achieve its objective. You may need to socialise with your teammates to create harmony. If an individual is not working up to par, the alternative is that you will have to work harder to make up for the shortcomings in order for the team to succeed i.e. you will need to put in extra time and effort to achieve the overall objective. It will be best if everyone can work extra hard together to achieve the goals and objectives with greater ease and even ahead of schedule.

良好的團隊關係可以讓
事情變得簡單可及。你需
要與你的團隊成員通過平常
社交相處來創造和諧，如果有
一個人不懂得團結配合，
你就需要更努力地工作來
彌補。例如，你要額外
付出更多的努力來達到
總體目標，如果每個人都
付出多一些，那麼達到目標
也會變得越來越容易，相信
也會提早完成目標了。

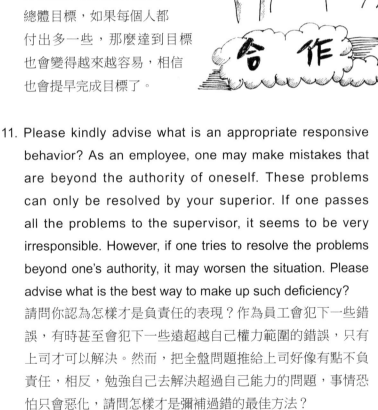

11. Please kindly advise what is an appropriate responsive behavior? As an employee, one may make mistakes that are beyond the authority of oneself. These problems can only be resolved by your superior. If one passes all the problems to the supervisor, it seems to be very irresponsible. However, if one tries to resolve the problems beyond one's authority, it may worsen the situation. Please advise what is the best way to make up such deficiency?

請問你認為怎樣才是負責任的表現？作為員工會犯下一些錯誤，有時甚至會犯下一些遠超越自己權力範圍的錯誤，只有上司才可以解決。然而，把全盤問題推給上司好像有點不負責任，相反，勉強自己去解決超過自己能力的問題，事情恐怕只會惡化，請問怎樣才是彌補過錯的最佳方法？

Everyone makes mistakes. If your superior is the only one who can resolve the mistakes, then you must inform your superior. This is not being irresponsible. This is the right thing to do since your supervisor is the only one who can resolve the problem. Admit to the problem and face the situation. The problem must be resolved at the earliest possible time. Delay will only make the problem worse. Send an apology to your supervisor and hope the situation can be resolved with minimal damage to the company.

每個人都會犯錯，如果是你上司才有權做決定的，你必須告知你的上司，這不是推卸責任，因為只有這樣你的上司才能解決這個問題，當然要承認你的問題/錯誤並面對造成的局面。問題需要在最快的時間內解決，拖延只會讓問題越來越差，向你的上司表達你的歉意，並希望問題能夠在影響最少的情況下解決。

12. As far as I understand, office politics can affect the future development of the employee. Is silence the best way to deal with office politics? I do worry that if I keep silent, I may have missed the opportunity to be noticed by my supervisor. Office politics causes damages within the company and will not do any good. As part of the management team, how will you deal with such a problem?

據我所知，辦公室政治會影響員工在公司的日後發展。請問沉默是不是最佳的方法？然而我擔心沉默會使自己難以被上司注重。此外，辦公室政治會造成內耗，對公司百害而無一利，請問你作為管理層如何解決這問題？

Silence is one of the ways to handle office politics. Try not to be involved in office politics. Either side will not like you, regardless, so it is best not to be involved. You can focus on your work and duties. That will be best. If you work hard and complete your work ahead of others, your boss will notice you. Office politics is unavoidable in many organisations but management can use it to its advantage, as some bosses prefer to have office politics in order to create competition between staff. It can work to your advantage or disadvantage.

保持沉默是處理辦公室政治的其中一種辦法，最好不要被涉及其中，因為始終會有一方不喜歡被你無視，所以最好的辦法是兩不參與。你要關注的是你的工作和責任，如果你努力工作並且提前完成你的工作，你的老板會注意到你。要獲得老板的關注並不需要通過辦公室政治的。辦公室政治在很多機構都難以避免，但管理人士也會利用它的特點，有些老板喜歡在公司內有某程度的辦公室政治，因為這樣才可以使員工間構成競爭。這可以是好處，同時也有其壞處。

13. How does one deal with co-workers who have different personalities from you? How do you balance work and relationships with these individuals?

請問如果在工作上需要與性格不合的同事共事，如何平衡工作和同事間的關係？

I once had a similar circumstance at work. It is not a matter a choice but it is out of needs. You have to work with different people whether you like them or not. Focus on the work and the outcome of the process. You do not need to socialise with the individuals you do not like but you need to learn to work with them on the job. Likes or dislikes do not come into force at work or on the job.

我以前也有相同的經歷，這不是選擇的問題，是必要的。你必須要與不同性格的人工作，不論你喜不喜歡他們，關鍵在於你和他的工作和成果。如果你不喜歡他們，你不需要與他們社交，但你必須和他們一起工作，喜不喜歡是不能帶到工作上的。

14. Will leadership concepts and culture spread more to Asian companies? Lots of young people have been frustrated with work because of their bosses and how they treat their staff. This has definitely induced a lot of fear and misconceptions on leadership concepts. The younger generation will reach more senior levels soon. Will it be possible that bosses can improve upon their leadership?

領袖才能思維和文化能否在亞洲的公司發揮作用呢？很多年輕人都很拼命工作，但因老板的工作方式和對待員工的方式，使年輕人工作時很沮喪，這直接導致員工對上級有一定的恐懼心理，而因此產生很多對領導觀感的誤解。其實年輕一代也會在很快的將來成為高層管理人士，老板們可否學習多一些領導才能的思維呢？

Leadership exists in the Asian culture, which happens to differ from the western culture. It takes a different approach to staff and businesses. To some people, it works better than others. I had the experience of taking a very friendly approach with my staff when I was working for a foreign company. My staff performed well. When I changed my job to work for a Hong Kong company, I found that I needed to use other forms of approach i.e. both friendly and strict approaches were necessary to achieve my objectives. Therefore, I only can conclude that one needs different approaches when one is at work and it totally depends on the person I am dealing with. I am sure that different youngsters require different incentives in order for them to work efficiently. There is no single set of rules on how to manage this. Your boss has reached where he/she is for a reason. That is why they are your boss, and not you. Learn from them so that you can use those skills in the future when you become a boss. They must have some good qualities that got them to where they are now. Not everyone can be a boss or leader; and we should give him or her more credit.

在亞洲文化中，領袖才能思維是普遍存在的，但與西方文化的領袖才能思維有所不同。對某些人來講這種方式很好，但對其他人不大有用。我曾經在外國公司工作，那時我習慣與同事很友好的相處，而他們也能很好地完成我要求的工作。而後來，我進入到一間香港公司，我發現我要轉變我的工作方式才可完成任務，例如我要同時採用友好和嚴厲的方式。因此我認為上司要在不同的工作環境和情況中，選擇不同的工作模式。不同的年輕人需要用不同的激勵方式才能有好的工作效果，沒有一個萬能的管理方法。你的領導或者老板也是通過他們的能力才做到現在的位置，這也是之所以他是你的老板。學習他們好的方面，這樣將來你成為領導者的時候也能善用。不是所有人都能成為老板或者領導者，你需要給他們一定的肯定。

15. I found out that criticisms and accusations seem to have become a very important driving force in life nowadays. After being criticised, many people are left feeling frustrated and unwilling to change their situation. Isn't life about appreciation, looking ahead and improving our future?

我發現現今社會被指責是很普遍的，被指責以後，人總是會變得害怕和沮喪並且不想改變。難道生活不是應該要多欣賞並且向前看和改善未來嗎？

Constructive criticism is good. Criticism for the sake of criticising someone or discrediting someone is not good. We need to have more constructive ideas rather than be one who only makes accusations and criticisms. You can make a difference to the situation if your criticism is beneficial to others. Criticism is not intended for personal gain but for the greater good. One can always improve but one also needs to look at the bigger picture to change. Sometimes, no change is better than change and at other times greater change is needed. One needs to make changes progressively; otherwise it will upset the equilibrium of our society. Drastic and sudden changes can cause greater damage.

建設性的批評是有益的，如果只是為了批判而指責或者羞辱他人，這就不對了，我們要有更多建設性的想法，而不應該只知道批評。如果你的批評對他人是有益的，你的建議才會被接納。批評不是只為了你自己的利益，而是為了大多數人的利益。有時，不變反而比變更好，人要學會循序漸進的改變，否則會破壞整個社會的平衡，突然的改變可能會造成更大的傷害。

16. As you said earlier, one shall not stay in the same job for a long time when one is young. One may need to move onto more suitable jobs. How will an employer view such an employee? Will the new company hire someone like that?

How will one respond to a potential employer if asked?

之前聽梁教授你講過，年青時，唔可以長時間停留係一份工上，要係適當的時候跳槽，以擴闊體驗。但係作為老細會點樣睇咁嘅員工，新公司會請一個咁嘅人乜？作為打工仔，如被老板問到，又可以點樣答先會俾到一個滿意嘅答案呢？

When you find a job, you must be totally committed to the work. I mentioned that, when you feel that you are not learning anything new and when the circumstances permit, then you can consider moving to new heights, but this is not a must. Does the new role offer more financial benefits and better prospects? No employer will hire someone who intends to leave the company. If you cannot find opportunities in the new role, you should not leave your present job as you can still learn and move ahead in your current role.

當你找到一份工作之後，你一定要全心全意投入到這工作當中。我的意思是指當你覺得你再學不到新的東西時，當環境允許你做出改變或者可提升到一個新的層次，你可以考慮跳槽。但這並不是一定的，你要看這份新工作是不是可以讓你有更好的前景，以及你本身有無一定的經濟實力。沒有人願意請一個隨時想要跳槽的員工，如果你並沒有好的機會，那你應該要留在現有的崗位，同時想辦法學習和尋找職位的晉升機會。

17. In the next few years, will the construction industry go into recession? I heard from some of my school mates who work for consultancy firms that they have not been hiring and

there aren't any tenders for new projects in our company. How do you view the market in the next few years?

未來呢幾年，建築市場會唔會開始出現衰退，聽一些在顧問公司嘅同學講，現在請人少咗，而且好似過完年後我地公司都好似冇乜新的落標，想問黎緊呢幾年個市道會係點？

Every industry will experience setback, which is why one needs to improve oneself in anticipation for the downturn of any industry. No industry will continuously rise up. What goes up must come down. If you are good at what you do and dedicated to your company, your employer will know and you will not be the first to be laid off. There are still many projects in the pipeline but they require approval from our government and LEGCO. It seems that many new public works projects are on hold due to the approval process. Yet the private sector is still going strong. The key is that if you are good at what you do, you will always find a job.

每一個行業都有低潮的時候，這也是為什麼每個人都要提升自己來面對低潮，沒有哪個行業可以一直上升，有起就有落。如果你對公司有價值並且一直忠心為公司效力，你的老板會知道的，第一個要炒的人肯定不是你。有很多其他的工程項目正在籌備中，但需要我們的立法會批準財務安排，很多新的公共項目都在審批過程中，私營項目是有持續增長的，問題的關鍵在於你自己是否出色，只要你本身有料就一定會有人僱用你。

18. There are many suppliers in the Hong Kong construction industry. They all seem to come from the Mainland China.

Our company has interviewed a number of them. We found that in the self-climbing formwork trade, their working style is very different from Hong Kong. Some terminology is different which causes a lot of confusion during our meetings. However, the pricing from Chinese companies is a lot cheaper than Hong Kong companies. This may be the opportunity for them to get into the Hong Kong market. The cultural differences between Hong Kong and the Mainland may also cause some confusion. In the present construction sector in Hong Kong, are there any agents who can assist in the coordination? If not, will this be an opportunity for someone who knows both the Hong Kong and China market?

而家有好多供應商都好似係大陸公司。之前公司約見過幾間，係關於自動爬升板模發現佢地嘅個套工作方式同香港嘅好唔同，例如同一樣野大陸同香港嘅叫法都唔同，當時都搞出好多誤會。咁我覺得搵大陸公司報價係處於價錢相對香港公司便宜，而大陸公司可能想借此機會打入香港市場，大家各取所需，但可能文化唔同會有阻礙。其實而家香港建築行業，有冇類似代理公司來負責協調這些公司，如果冇，咁對於熟悉中港市場嘅人黎講會唔會係一條財路？

There are many companies that come to Hong Kong in order expand their business overseas. There are many Chinese construction companies already operating in Hong Kong. One needs to understand how both sides operate. When one evaluates a product, it needs to fit the purpose of the acquisition. It needs to meet the safety and quality requirements in Hong Kong. Surely if one understands both cultures, it will help in getting the right products. Before anyone can understand both sides, one needs to learn the trade practices in both Hong Kong and China. There are many agents for oversea products in Hong Kong. There are also agents for many Chinese products also. These people do exist in our industry.

有很多公司來香港是為了更方便走出海外，有很多中國的建築公司已經在香港營運中，一個人需要瞭解中港雙方是如何運作。當你評價一個產品時，它需要符合購買的需求，需要滿足香港的安全和質量的要求。當然，如果有中間人了解中港情況的，肯定更容易及有助於找到更合適的產品。想要了解兩地工作，要學習香港和中國雙方面的貿易知識。在香港有許多國外產品的代理，同時也有很多中國產品的代理，這些人都存在於我們建築行業內。

19. As a fresh graduate, should I join a small company or a large corporation? I have friend who joined a small company and his starting salary is higher and his prospects for promotion is also higher.

如果作為一個新畢業生，其實入D細公司做會好D定大公司好D？我有朋友係細公司做緊，起薪高升得快。

You may learn more in a smaller company as a fresh graduate but there is less job security. If the small company does not have work, you will be laid off. You will need to work twice as hard in a small company since you will be given the opportunity to be more responsible in your work. A small company has fewer means to train you and often you will have to learn on the job. I think if you are willing to work hard, you will survive in both. One should try different types of companies if given the opportunity. It is a new experience when you work for different companies. The only thing that remains the same is that you will need to work extremely hard.

作為一名新畢業生,可能你在小公司會學得更多,但工作的穩定性會相對比較風險高一些。如果小公司沒有生意,你會馬上被解僱,你而且需要在小公司工作加倍努力,因為你將被給予更多機會去做更多的工作,賦予更多責任。在小公司裏,結構性的培訓很少,你通常要在工作上學習。我認為,只要你願意努力工作,你在大小公司都能生存下去。有機會的話,你應該嘗試不同的公司,因為這樣可以提供新的經驗。唯一相同的是,你需要非常非常努力地工作。

20. What should a fresh graduate entering the workforce need to be aware of?

你認為剛畢業的大學生剛進入工作時需要注意些什麼?

You will need to be prepared to learn, to be sincere and acknowledge your weaknesses. You will need to work hard and fulfill the needs of your boss; and help your boss to accomplish his tasks. You must have initiative to learn, to ask questions and understand why certain things are done in a particular way in the company. You must follow up on matters with self-initiative and learn from your co-workers and explore outside the scope of your work.

你要準備學習，對工作要有真誠，承認自己的缺點，努力工作，滿足上司的要求，幫助你的老闆完成他的任務，必須主動學習，學習提問，搞清楚在公司為什麼有些事情要通過特定的方式去做，自發地跟進工作，向其他同事學習，不要僅限於自己的工作範圍內的事物。

21. What qualities do I need, as a fresh graduate, to get a job in property development?

你認為剛畢業的大學生進入一家房地產公司，需要具備哪些條件？

I am not sure that an engineer should start their career with a property developer. You may need more construction experience before going into a property development company. You will need the skills of negotiation; have the ability to communicate well with consultants on design issues, and knowledge of contracts. You will need the competence to supervise construction companies; and know where to source information, how to deal with government approvals etc. I trust these are skill sets that you will need to learn and acquire before you can be an effective Project Manager in a property development company.

我不認為一名工程師一開始應選擇一間房地產發展公司，你在進入一間地產發展公司之前應該要先擁有更多的地盤施工經驗。您會需要談判技巧，在設計問題上如何可以更好地與顧問公司溝通，合同上的認知，如何督促建築公司的能力，知道在哪裏尋找信息，知道如何處理與政府部門的批核等工作。我相信這些都是一些你會需要學習的技能，這樣你才能在地產發展公司裏發揮得更好，才能勝任成為一名出色的項目經理。

22. What does a fresh graduate entering into the workforce need to do in order to be successful?

你認為剛畢業的大學生進入社會後，若想成功，需要做哪方面的努力？

I think continuous learning and working hard are the two basic elements to reach success. You will need to have self-initiative to learn. No one can force you to learn but yourself. If you want to be successful, you have to gain enough experience and be able to achieve new heights through learning.

我認為不斷學習和努力工作是兩個基本要素。你需要有主動

學習的能力，沒有人會強迫你學習，如果你想達到新的境
界，你必須要有足夠的經驗並能夠通過學習來實現。

23. For an individual, do you think that one should stay in the
same job or try different types of jobs?

以一個人的工作而言，您認為是應該一如既往的堅持某一份
工作，還是嘗試不同的工作？

Fate will decide what you do. Initially, it is best to start and
focus on a single job. If you are the best in the field, you will
be successful. If you have fulfilled all your obligations in life
e.g. basic needs, family obligations etc., then you can move
into other areas of interests. You must fulfill your obligations
in life first. Focus is very important in life. You cannot work
on many things at the same time. You can only focus on
one single issue at any one time.

命運會決定你將來做什麼。開始時最好專注於單一的工作，
如果你在該領域是最好的，你一定會成功。如果你已經可以
滿足到生活的基本要求和家庭責任等，那麼你可以轉到你感
興趣的其他領域。但首先，你需要有一定的基礎，滿足生活
上的需要和責任，這是很重要的。你不能在同一時間上做許
多事情，你在每一時段，應該專注於一件單一的問題上。

24. I currently run a trading business doing trade across
Malaysia and Hong Kong. What is your advice on working in
full-time employment and running one's own business at the
same time?

我目前在馬來西亞有一個貿易生意，經營香港和馬來西亞的

貿易。你對同時做一份全職的工作和有自營的生意,意見如何?

You will need to be focused. You need to be totally dedicated in a full time job. Having another business on the side will distract you from your work. You cannot do well in your business at the same time, as a business requires just as much commitment and dedication. You will need to work very hard to ensure successful outcomes.

你需要專注做好你的工作,每一份工作都是需要你全身心投入的,同時做自己的生意會讓你分心,這樣你兩樣都做不好。生意需要全面承諾和投入,你要非常努力工作才能成功。

25. Will I have to work in Mainland China to get a good job?
   我會不會需要到國內才能有一份好的工作?

For the younger generation, in the next 30 years, I believe that you must be prepared to work in China. This is where the economic growth is happening. If you do not need to work in China now, you will never know when you will need to go work in China. All employers will expect their employees to be prepared to go to China anytime since the company will probably acquire work in China sooner or later.

對於你們這一代來講,未來的三十年裏,我相信你們一定要做好去國內工作的準備。中國是經濟發展最快的國家,即使你現在不需要去國內工作,將來有一天你還是會要去的。所有僱主都會希望他的僱員可以做好去國內的準備,因為說不準他什麼時候就會需要人去國內工作。

26. Should I start my own company?

我應該自己開公司嗎？

Essentially, one needs to gain enough knowledge to start one's own company. You can learn from other people's mistakes. You will need to have saved your first bucket of gold. Starting you own company can mean liability. You need to hire people and invest in capital; that is a liability. You need to have sufficient working capital to run your company. You need to have a good marketing plan for your products or services. You need to know where and who are your clients. One needs to prepare for a new business, otherwise you will learn the hard way. It may be easy to start but it is often difficult to keep it sustainable. Plan before you start and do not do things irrationally.

首先，你要有足夠的知識來開始你自己的公司，要從他人的錯誤中吸取經驗。你首先要儲夠第一桶金，開設自己的公司意味着承擔責任，你要僱用員工和投資貨品，要有足夠的營運資本。你要對自己的產品或者服務對象有好的市場計劃，你要知道你的目標客戶是誰和在哪裏，你要為你要做的事業做好準備，否則你只會通過失敗來積累經驗。要開始很容易，但要好好維持是很困難的，開始前做好計劃，千萬不要做一時衝動之決策。

27. How can I develop good relationships with colleagues in the workplace?

我在公司裏要如何和同事建立好關係？

Firstly, you will need to be nice to all of your colleagues. It needs to come from the heart. People can tell if you are sincere or not. You must always try to learn from your colleagues and every one of them is your teacher. Learn only the good of others and forget the bad. Secondly, appreciate the things they do and try to help your colleagues wherever possible. This will get you a long way if put into real practice.

首先，你要真心地對你的同事友好，他們會很容易分辨出你是真誠還是虛偽的。你要向每一個同事學習，每個同事都可以是你的老師，學習他們好的一面，忘記不好的一面。欣賞他人做的事，也要經常幫助他人。這樣實踐下去，才會使你和你的同事有長遠友好的關係。

28. What is the construction market like in Hong Kong?
香港的建築行業發展怎樣？

Hong Kong has a very buoyant construction industry. It has it's ups and downs with workload but I trust it is one of the best markets for construction. Hong Kong has many interesting and challenging projects. Every project is unique in nature and you will always face different challenges. It is not for the faint-hearted but for a fast-moving and decisive person.

香港的建築行業發展十分蓬勃。這個市場的工作量有起有落，但我相信在建築行業来講，香港是一個十分好的地方。香港有很多有意思及具挑戰性的項目，每個項目都是獨一無二的，你總會遇到不同的挑戰。香港建築行業不適合一名膽小的人，但是很適合一名有膽量和決斷力強的人。

29. What was your first work experience in civil engineering like? Compared with academic work, did you ever feel powerless or did you attain more? How did you deal with that?
相比你在土木工程的第一份工作經驗是怎樣的？與學術性的教學，你感覺到是更有成就感還是更無力感？你是怎樣處理這種情緒呢？

My first work experience went well and I learnt a lot from my supervisor. As a matter of fact, I called him about a year ago to thank him for teaching me so much and for shaping me into what I have become today. He was so pleased and happy and this is after 38 years since we last spoke. So, we finally met up for dinner in Hong Kong and we shared our life experiences for the past 38 years over 6 hours! He was someone who I needed to thank and it is always good to thank someone when you still can. Work experience and academic study are very different. One can do well in both. Your needs in life will drive you to work harder. You will achieve through accomplishment. My academic teaching is intended with a purpose to share my knowledge and experience with the younger generation and I hope that they can learn more and achieve new heights. Hopefully they can achieve a higher plateau and they can contribute to our society in a meaningful and productive manner. I feel happy when one achieves their objectives in work and when I know my students can learn from me. I trust working on teaching has its unique form of happiness and personally, I like both. I have never felt powerless in life. I only believe that one can always achieve new heights if you work hard enough. It is important that if one tries their best, one will not regret. It is not a matter of achievement or how much you achieve but you must answer to yourself and know you have tried your best. It is important to live a life with no regrets.

我第一份在加拿大工作的經歷很好，我從當時的主管那裏學到很多東西。事實上，我一年前曾特別打了個電話給他，並且感謝他對我以前的幫助和指導，讓我成為今天的我，他也十分之高興，這自從我們上一次交談已經是38年了。我們最終有機會一起在香港吃晚餐，並且分享了這38年來的人生經歷，交談了整整六個小時。他是一位讓我想起，我需要說聲感謝的人。工作經驗和教學理論是很不同的，有些人可以在兩方面都很優秀。你對人生的需求往往會使你更加努力地工作，你會通過工作的成就而得到一定的滿足感。學術教學可使我讓年輕的一代分享我的知識和經驗，希望他們能夠從分享中有所獲得而更上一層樓，希望年青人可以通過我的教導而得到幫助，甚至做到比我更出色的成績，同時可以對社會做更多的事情和貢獻，這樣我會非常高興。我個人認為這是一種不同的快樂，我個人對這兩種不同的成就（工作上和教學上）都喜歡。我一生中從未覺得有無能為力的時候，我覺得一個人只要努力工作就一定可以達到新的目標。最重要的是要盡了最大的努力，那麼你就沒有遺憾的地方。這並不是成就的問題，也不是你獲得多少，而是要問問自己你有沒有盡力而為，無悔對你的一生更為重要。

30. Did you find it more meaningful to work in a specific job role like consultants, contractors etc.?
你認為某些工作種類會否更有意義？例如做工程顧問工作，或承包商等？

Work itself is not about it being meaningful or not. One needs to work in order to fulfill life obligations. One needs to be productive towards society. One cannot rely upon another to survive. One needs to be independent. Work provides you with a good living so you are able to enjoy life. Work provides opportunities for you to help others. Regardless of which job role or category you work in, it is important that you can contribute to the company you work for and assist your boss to achieve his tasks. Work only becomes meaningful when it satisfies your needs. Your needs can be monetary, or about learning experiences, opportunities to explore new things, standard of living etc.

工作不是關乎有沒有意義的，每個人需要工作來滿足生活上的需求，要對社會有建設性，一個人是不可以依賴他人而活的，需要獨立。工作可以提供給你足夠的生活需要，從而能享受生活。工作也給你機會去幫助他人。不論從事哪種工作，重要的是你能對公司有所作為，幫助你的上司完成他交待的任務。當然工作能滿足你的需求，它就是有意義的。你的需求可能是金錢，學習經驗，有機會探索新事物，或舒適生活等等。

31. What does a change of role mean to you? For example when becoming a chartered engineer or landing a promotion? Have you ever felt you have done "enough"?

角色的改變對你而言意味着什麼？例如做一名特許工程師或升職？你有沒有到達到一個階段你覺得已經足夠了？

Change of roles will improve your social standing, bring better monetary return and recognition for the achievements in certain qualifications in life; which will provide opportunities for your career advancement. There are times in life that you do not need further recognition e.g. another chartered membership, but one does need to progress otherwise one will be left behind. The society is progressing and it always will. One needs to keep up with progress. One may feel tired at times but that only means you just need to rest before you go on again. There are always plenty of opportunities in life but it is up to you to decide whether to accept the next challenge or not.

角色改變可以改進你的社會地位，更好的財富收入，對你的成就和資歷肯定的認可，提供下一步發展的機會和基礎。你在人生中有時不需要有更多的認可，如另一個勛章或另一資歷認可等，但人是需要進步的，否則你就會被淘汰。社會永遠在進步，每個人都要跟着發展的步伐。可能有時會覺得疲憊，但休息一會兒之後，還是要繼續前行。生活中總是有很多機會，你要自己決定是否接受下一個挑戰。

32. When did the idea of entrepreneurship begin for you? How did you find the resources like staff and interpersonal networks etc.?

你的創業精神是什麼時候開始出現的？你是怎樣拿到資源，如僱員、人脈等？

One needs to be well equipped before one can be an entrepreneur. You need the resources, the knowledge, the networks, and the right market condition before one can begin. I learnt through my own work experience; and I got to know the industry well. I saved up for my first bucket of gold; and I knew which market I wanted to enter and I got to know where to find help if needed. Selecting your business sector is important. Learn from other's mistakes and get to know the people in your sector or industry. Be careful with spending and cost control. Be conservative in your investment. Find a mentor where possible.

要成為一名企業家，你首先要武裝自己。你要有資源、知識、網絡和合適的市場環境。我是從我的工作經驗中學到的，我了解到行業的運作，我儲到第一桶金，我知道要做哪個行業及市場，知道如果有需要可以去哪裏尋求幫助。選擇你要做的行業很重要，要從別人的失敗中吸取教訓，認識行業裏有用的人，對開銷和成本控制要特別小心，不要貿然投資，以保守為上，最好能找到一個好的導師。

33. In view of the technological advancement, how does your expectation of the graduates joining your company change? What personal characteristics encourage you to provide them with more advanced training?

考慮到現代科技發展，你對進入到你公司的畢業生有什麼期待？具有怎樣個人特徵的人會讓你更有興趣提供更多的培訓機會給他？

With technological changes, one needs to know new skills and one needs to learn new skills; hence one needs to obtain the necessary skills to adapt to any company changes. One needs to quickly adapt to new changes. One needs to be flexible and willing to learn. One needs to work hard. One needs to react quickly. One needs to have the initiative to respond and act. One must take self-initiative to follow up and complete assignments.

隨着現今技術的進步，你要知道新的技術，也要能夠學習新技術，要明白哪種技能是公司需要的，要能獲得必要的技能來適應公司方向的改變。每個人還需要接受新的改變，要靈活處理，願意學習，努力工作，反應迅速，主動回應改變，能自發地安排跟進工作，完成任務。

34. From your work experience, what makes civil engineering a profession? Perhaps it appears challenging? How have technological advancement contributed to the productivity of civil engineering?

從你的工作經驗來看，什麼條件可以使土木工程成為一門專業，或許看上去有些挑戰性？技術上的演變如何對土木工程的生產力有所貢獻？

Civil Engineering provides a lot of challenges for anyone who is working in the industry. There are always new challenges. One needs to work very hard. One needs to be prepared to work in adverse conditions. One needs to create new methods to perform different tasks. One will need to handle crisis management. Technology can only assists engineers to improve their productivity and efficiency. One needs to determine which of these technologies actually fit the needs before implementation. There are many technologies available but it is important to understand the suitability in purpose before implementation. Sometimes, it may only add to cost and wastage.

土木工程這個行業為每一個在這行工作的人都提供一定的挑戰，永遠都有新的挑戰，每個人都要非常努力地工作，要準備在最艱難的條件下工作，要準備隨時用最新的方式來完成不同的任務，要懂得危機處理。技術只能協助工程師改善他們的生產力和效率，要先判斷這個技術是否真的適合行業應用。現有很多新技術，但應用前，首要是理解其是否符合需求，因為有時可能只會增加了成本和造成浪費。

35. Technically, how do you perceive the adoption of 3D printing into civil engineering, like for efficient building processes? What are the possible aspects that will drive 3D printing in construction in future research e.g. stability, material usage etc.?

技術上，你怎樣理解3D打印在土木工程中的應用，會否增加建築施工過程的效率？3D打印建造，有哪方面可作研究？

I am not sure the benefits of 3D printing will bring much benefits to civil engineering. It can produce a sample/mock up for the works but it cannot be mass-produced. There are many repetitive works in civil engineering and 3D rendering may be too slow and time consuming. Even though the sample/mock up may be able to assist in various testing environments e.g. wind tunnel testing, water wave testing etc., one can probably use it for simulation works only. In actual works onsite, I think its use will be limited. I think demand will determine what future research is needed. I think 3D printing is restricted to use in the lab and not beyond. You can always create different structures from 3D printing and test it in the lab to improve structural design and efficiency.

我不確定3D打印對土木工程科會有很大的好處，它可以幫助創造一個好的樣板，但它不能大量生產。在土木工程通常有很多重復性的工作，3D可能會太慢，花費時間太長。不過你還是可以用樣板來做不同的測試，例如風洞測試，浪潮測試等等。你可能可以用在仿真測試上，但不一定能在現實工作環境上應用。我覺得它的功效會有一定的限制，需求會決定它的未來研究方向，我覺得它只限於實驗室使用。你可以用3D創造不同的結構並在實驗室進行測試，這樣可以更有效的提高結構設計和效益。

36. This is my fifth year in this industry. I think that the community does not really know what engineers do in Hong Kong. When people think about building construction or property development, they just know of the Architect and no one seems to know that there are other roles called Structural Engineer/ Civil Engineer/ Geotechnical Engineer. They cannot distinguish the differences between them. I do think that the community should know more about this industry since some young people may want to join this industry, but only very few of them know that they can be an engineer or an architect. Just like me, I did badly in high school and had to select lower down my list of choices in my JUPAS list. I never thought of civil engineering since I didn't know anything about it, so I put it on the bottom of my JUPAS list. Finally, I took this course and enjoy it very much. My situation may only be one of the many examples. There are very few options and opportunities at the universities in Hong Kong. How can the government change this situation? We need more people to know about engineers.

這是我在這個行業的第五年，我覺得香港人對工程師並不是很了解。當人想到建築或者土地開發的時候，他們只會想到建築師，但沒有人知道還有其他的職位叫結構工程師/土木工程師/地質工程師等。他們不能分辨出每個角色的不同。我覺得社會上有必要了解更多，因為有些年輕人或許會希望加入這個行業，但只有少部分人知道他們除了做建築師之外還可以做工程師。就像我，我高中時成績很差，選擇工程作為最終行業，我從沒考慮過做土木工程師，因為我根本不知道這行業是什麼。但最終我讀了這門課程並且感到非常有興趣。我的情況可能只是其中一個案例，香港的大學只有很少的選項，政府要怎樣讓這個情況有所改變呢？我們需要有更多的人知道工程師。

The community has very little knowledge about engineers. I think the Hong Kong Institution of Engineers (HKIE) is more focused on the development and the interests of the engineers but has done little promotion on the engineering profession itself. Engineers are less involved in politics and consultative committees of the government. I think more self-promotion for engineers is needed. I trust other engineers commonly share your observation and sentiments. I will certainly reflect your views to our engineering representative in LEGCO and to the President of the HKIE. This is important to us all. Engineers' contribute immensely to our community and this cannot be ignored for the HKIE bears the major responsibility on this matter. In actual fact, many engineers work within the government. Engineers are only less known in the community but they are well known within the government. I agree that more promotion is definitely necessary. As fellow engineers, we all need to take up this responsibility.

公眾對於工程師的認知了解很少，我想香港工程師學會只關注工程師的興趣和發展，但對於工程師職業的推廣卻很少。工程師很少涉及政治和咨詢委員會，我覺得還有很多事情可以做，以幫助工程師推廣自己。我相信你講的經歷很普遍，我一定會向立法會代表工程系的議員和香港工程師學會主席反映你的意見。這對我們所有工程師都很重要。工程師對社會的作用毋庸置疑，學會應該對這個問題負上重要責任。事實上，現在很多工程師在政府工作，工程師在社會上很少人知，但在政府內是很多人知道的。我同意你的觀點，推廣是很必須的，而且每一個工程師也有這責任。

37. With reference to my question above, I think the community does not respect Engineers as one of the main professions. Engineers ensure the safety of buildings and civil structures and this saves a lot of lives. But we do not have equal rewards as doctors. I refer to the recent consultancy fees from developers. I feel like they are humiliating the Engineers. I think they need to pay reward and more respect to the importance of Engineers in the development process. However, the community does not understand our role and only a few respect us. How can we turn this situation around?

我之所以會有以上的問題是因為我認為社會上並不是很尊重工程師，也不視之為專業人士，而僅僅是視之為一門職業。工程師保證了很多建築物和土木結構的安全，這一點已經挽救了很多生命，但我們並沒有與之對等的榮譽和回報像醫生等。參考最近開發商給工程師的顧問費，我感覺他們是在羞辱工程師。在我看來，他們沒有意識到工程師在項目上的重要性。這是因為整個社會都不甚了解我們的角色，只有少部分人尊重我們，我們應該怎樣改變這樣的情況呢？

Respect can only be earned. In Hong Kong, we have built some of the greatest structures/bridges in the world, only that it is less known within our community except within the engineering profession. I agree that this is not enough and we must do more about this. Remuneration can only come with respect in the profession and ultimately, we need to earn it. I agree many developers do not respect professionals. It is also perhaps our fault that there is always an architect or an engineer who is willing to accept such low fees. Naturally, recommended schedule of fees is available but this is never used in practice. It is up to engineers and professionals to ensure reasonable fees are being received. There will always be a willing party who is willing to accept low fees and surely, this is bad for business and may even affect the professional integrity of the profession.

尊重是靠自己贏回來的。我們在香港確實建造了很多全球認同的偉大建築物/工程項目/橋樑等等，但除了在工程界別內，只有很少普通市民知道。我也認為現在很多開發商不太尊重專業人士，不過這也有我們的責任，因為總有一些建築師或工程師願意接受很低的價格提供專業服務。事實上價格是有一定的標準建議價格的，但從來沒有實在地執行過。這只可由工程師和專業人士們，自行判斷是否收到合理的價格。總會有一方願意接受低的價格，而這樣將會對整個行業造成一定的破壞性，甚至影響到行業的公信力。

38. The Buildings Department controls a central data bank, which lists all the building materials that can be used without any special approval (as they are already approved by the technical section of The Buildings Department). However, this data bank does not seem to be updated, even though some of the new technologies were approved previously in other projects. If one uses the materials that are not stated in the data bank, it will require a much longer approval process by the technical section. Hence, we always hesitate to use these technologies such as the new HILTI products. This makes the industry stagnant and lacking improvement for years. How can we force the government to put some effort into this?

屋宇署有中央數據庫寫明瞭哪些建築材料是我們可以應用，而不需要通過屋宇署的特殊批準程序，但是他們卻從來沒有更新過數據庫，尤其是有很多新的技術可能已在其他項目已有批準和應用過的。這樣導致一旦使用沒有列在中央數據庫裏的材料，就要經過很長的時間由其技術部門來審批，因此，我們總是猶豫使用新的技術，如有些新的喜利得產品等，這讓整個行業這些年來都沒有好好的發展和改進。我們怎樣能讓政府認知到這一個問題而做出改善呢？其實只是需要更新數據庫裏的數據而已。

I agree with your observation. I trust the HKIE can highlight these issues to the government. HKIE needs to be proactive in making change for the industry. Most government officials are apprehensive towards change because change means risk, and a risk which they do not want to take responsibility for. That is why there are so little changes made to specifications for years. If you have real case examples, please provide them to me and I shall contact relevant parties and try to make some changes for the betterment of our industry.

我同意你的觀點，我相信工程師學會可以向政府強調這些問題，工程師學會需要主動改變現狀。大多數政府官員畏於改變，因為改變意味着可能有一定的風險，而他們不想承擔這樣的責任。這也是為什麼這麼多年來，改變的只是一小部分。如果你有實際案例，請提供給我，我會盡力傳遞給相關部門，試着做一些對我們行業有益的改善。

39. How can we make employers respect their employees like in Europe, in regards to working hours? It would be shocking for someone to work for 12 hours or more in Europe. However, it is very common in Hong Kong and employers think it is a norm. Some bosses even think it is given that their employees do overtime work (which is unpaid). In my view, the present society and our generation do not agree with this.

我們應該怎樣才可以讓僱主更尊重他們的員工，像歐洲那樣？我是指工作時間方面，對比歐洲，每天工作12個小時是極其可怕的，但是在香港這是很普遍的，而僱主認為這很正常，有些老板甚至認為不加班的員工是有問題的（無薪酬的加班）。就我的觀察，現今社會和我們這一代人都不贊同這種看法。

I believe all employers must respect their employees since the employees help their employers earn their profits. An employee can establish himself as irreplaceable i.e. the employer can't do without you. One needs to continuously improve oneself and do more. One needs to work beyond your own responsibilities i.e. do more than your scope of work. This will make you more valuable than your other colleagues. That will make you irreplaceable to your boss.

I agree working 12 hours or more is not reasonable. I hope that you are learning from such long hours of working. I think if you are learning then you are gaining. Once you feel that you had learnt all that you can, then it may be time to move on in your life unless the situation changes. You could also find the opportunity to express your views to your

supervisor. I think sometimes reasonable overtime work may be necessary in order for Hong Kong to thrive competitively but it does not mean bosses can overwork their staff. Staff will have a lower productivity if they are overworked and exhausted. I never expected my staff to work overtime but I demanded them to complete specific tasks within a reasonable timeframe. Your supervisor knows who works harder than others and he will provide promotion opportunity to the concerned staff who works harder. If he does not reward good workers, then he is not a good boss. I always feel that reasonableness is required in the relationship between employers and employees. If there are urgent matters, the whole company should pitch in and work to address the issue. Hence, the company also needs to be reasonable to their staff. The younger generation sometime do not realise the necessity of working hard since they never experienced downturn in their career or economy. They will learn the hard way and some of them will be replaced if they do not appreciate that Hong Kong needs to maintain competitive. Otherwise our competitors like Singapore and China will be ahead of us and we will be left behind. This will then cause drop in salaries and will diminish our standard of living and quality of life.

我認為所有的僱主都應該尊重他的員工，因為員工是幫他們賺取利潤的。一個員工應該要讓他自己變得是不可取代的，也就是說僱主非你不可。員工應該要持續地進步及完善自己，做出成績。做事不應該僅限於自己的職責範圍，而要擴大你的工作範圍，這樣會讓你比起其它的員工更有價值，從而使你變得不可取代。我也認為每天工作12個小時是不合理的，我希望你在工作中學到新的經驗，如果你學到了新的事物，你就有新的收獲，一旦你覺得學夠了，可能便是改變的時候了。你要先找機會向你的上司表達你自己看法，有時加班工作是必須的，因為要保持香港的競爭力，但這並不是說要員工過度地工作。如果員工太累了，員工的生產力反而會降低。我從不指望我的員工加班工作，但我希望他們能在合理的時間內完成所有任務。你的上司會知道誰更勤力,同時他也會給勤力的員工更多的升職機會,如果他不獎勵這些努力工作的員工,那他就不是一個好上司。我覺得僱主與員工的關係要雙方合理,如果真的有緊急的工作,公司應該上下齊心去解決問題。年輕一代通常不太理解努力工作的意義,因為他們從沒有經歷過經濟低迷的困境。他們應該要回顧香港那段困難的歲月,要知道現在的香港得來不易,如果不努力保持我們的競爭力,我們隨時會被取代。如新加坡,中國,都會超越過我們,這會導致薪金下滑,並且降低我們在香港的生活水平和質量。

40. I want to resign and join another company. However, in the new role, I will be working for a competitor. What reasons can I provide my current boss so as ensure a smooth exit? Of course I do not hold any important or classified documents.

當我想辭職加入另一家公司,而這間公司與我現有的公司是競爭對手,我應該怎樣告訴我現在的公司,以免產生不良的反應呢?當然我手中並沒有任何公司的機密信息。

You do not need any reasons to resign. You just resign and tender your notice of resignation. All you have to say is that you need to move on but you want to give proper notice and conduct a formal handover of your duties and responsibilities. Life does not end with resignation from a job. If you are friends with your co-workers, they will still be your friends.

你不需要任何理由來辭職的,只是辭職而已。你要說的是,你需要繼續向前看,但你要妥當地移交你的工作和責任,人生不會因辭職而結束，如果你與同事們是朋友，辭職後他們仍然是你的朋友。

41. If some lower grade workers who are not under my direct management refuse to do their job or are out of control, what should I do?

如果在公司里低級別的同事（但不屬於我主管的）拒絕工作或者不受控制，我應該怎樣做？

If he or she has a supervisor, you must go through his or her supervisor so as to instruct them to get the job done. If he or she is under your supervision then you can issue a warning. If he or she continues to refuse work and is out of control, you have the choice of dismissing him or her. However, you must discuss this with the Human Relations department in your company before any move shall be made. I trust a warning is good enough and needed. Also, discuss with him or her some of the reasons why they don't want to do certain jobs or why they lose control. Use your listening skills; he or she may have a good reason to refuse the work so always find out beforehand.

如果他有主管，你必須通過他的主管指導他做工作。如果他在你的監督下，你就要警告他，如果他繼續失去控制，你可以選擇開除他。你必須與人力資源部門先討論此事，然後才能採取任何行動。 我相信最初只需要一個好好的警告，與他討論一下，他為什麼不想做某些工作或失去控制的原因。你要好好地聆聽他的話，他可能有拒絕工作的正當理由，先找到這個基本原因，再做決定。

42. If there are 3 companies to choose from where one can provide a better mentor but a lower salary, one may have a chance for chartered membership but a lower salary and one is my current job with no apparent support for months, how should I decide for my future?

如果我面前有三家公司，其中一家可以為我提供一個很好的導師，但薪水較低；另一個是較低的工資，但有機會拿到我的工程專業資格；以及我目前的公司，幾個月來仍然沒有任何支持，我該如何對我的將來做決定？

At different points of your life, you will work for different companies. At present, I think one of your main objectives is to get chartered membership. Therefore, I recommend you first get chartered since it will raise your salary. There is always a mentor around the corner in your life. Once you get chartered, then you can find a good mentor to guide you along.

你在人生的不同階段可以去不同的公司。目前，我相信你的主要目標是先拿到你的專業資格，所以我建議你先去拿專業資格，這樣會獲得更高的報酬。在你人生中有很多時刻會出現好的導師，一旦你拿到專業資格後，你就可以找好的導師來引導你的未來。

43. How do you avoid trends that you don't want to follow?
如何避免那些你不想跟隨的趨勢？

You always have a choice to be yourself. No one can determine your future. You are the only one who can determine your own destiny. You control your future in your own hands. You do not need to follow any trends. You can create your own trend.

你可選擇離開並維持自己，沒有人可以決定你的未來，除了你自己。你的將來控制在你自己的手裏，不需要隨波逐流，你應該自己決定未來的道路。

44. What's your view on the development of Information Technology in Hong Kong?
你如何看待香港電訊行業的發展？

Development in research, high-end products and support to industries should be the future areas of development for information technology in Hong Kong.
電訊高端產品，電訊研發和電訊對產業的支援及維護，是香港電訊業的未來發展趨勢。

45. What's your view on the development of smart phone applications?
你如何看待智能手機應用程式未來的發展？

There are already many people working in this field. It has a low entry barrier. If the applications are for our next generation, there are still opportunities. The applications need to cater to the needs of society such as convenience to users or for the elderly.

已經有很多人在這個領域發展，這領域的入門檻不高。如果
這個應用程式是為我們下一代的， 那麼它仍有機會。應用程
式應該要迎合社會需求，例如幫助老年人的，一定要方便使
用。

46. What is the prospect for Engineering in Hong Kong?
香港工程學的前景如何？

Engineering teaches one how to think logically and how to
resolve problems. It will give you a good start to your career.
You will need to learn more than engineering in life. Many
engineers move onto other professions while others stay in
engineering for their whole life. I think Hong Kong has many
opportunities for engineers. We have one of the biggest
engineering markets in the world (China) just around the
corner. This is a market that we cannot ignore. We as
engineers can contribute in many ways to both Hong Kong
and China.

工程科是教導大家如何用邏輯思考問題和如何解決問題，它
作為你事業的起步是很有幫助的。作為一名工程師，你要在
一生中學習除了工程科以外的更多知識。工程只可以為你的
事業提供一個好的基礎，很多工程師在人生不同階段會轉換
到其它的專業領域，同時也有很多工程師會一輩子專注於工
程科。我認為香港能提供工程師很好的環境和很多的機會，
我們擁有世界上最大的市場 "中國" 作為我們的後盾，這是
我們不可錯過的市場，我們作為工程師可以在香港和中國國
內做出很多的貢獻。

47. What's your view on the establishment of the Innovation and Technology Bureau in Hong Kong?
你對成立創新及科技局有什麼看法？

This is a good beginning for Hong Kong but there is still plenty of work that needs to be done. It needs to work with industries to create worthy contribution to our society. It is something that the government is trying to create and it requires the right people to get it going.
這是一個好的開始，但仍有很多工作要做，需要與行業互相結合才能對社會有所貢獻。政府正在試圖做這方面的工作，但它需要合適的人才方能成功。

48. How do you prioritize between rules and flexibility in the work place? I was criticized by others to say that 'rules are rigid but humans are flexible'. I understand the person who criticized me wants me to be more flexible. However, I believe that for a company to operate properly, rules are needed. This applies to Hong Kong whereby most of the people are law abiding, which makes Hong Kong prosper. I also believe that if there is a practice of breaking rules, it can cause much trouble for the company. I would like to know is there a balance between the two? Please kindly advice.
請問您會如何在變通跟規則之間作出取捨？我曾經被人批評"規則係死既，人係生既"，我明白批評我的人是希望我變通，可是，我認為要有效運作一間公司，規則是不可或缺的。正如香港之所以會繁榮，是因為大部分人都守法。我認為變通就是打破規則的做法，處理不善可能會為公司帶來很多麻煩。因此，我希望知道有沒有平衡兩者的方法。

Rules are man made. You will need to find the balance between rules and being flexible. You will need to follow rules since the rules are not made by you but by the company. If you want to make changes to the rules, you must consult your boss first. If he agrees, then it will be acceptable to change. I do not think you have the authority to change rules at random. Ask before you act.

規則是人創造出來的，你要在規則和靈活變通之間取得平衡。你需要按規矩行事因為這是由你的公司製定出來的，而不是你。如果你想要改變規則，你先要和你的老板商量，如果他同意的話，改變是可以的。我不認為你有權隨意改變規則，所以改動前一定要先咨詢。

49. Do you think Hong Kong is a good place to establish Information Technology businesses?
你認為香港適合發展電訊行業嗎？

It depends. Hong Kong is a good bridge to connect with the rest of the world. It is also a good place to protect your intellectual property rights. It may be good to market your products overseas. It also depends what you are creating. It may be cheaper to do it in China. One needs to combine the efforts in China and Hong Kong to effectively reach the rest of the world.

這要根據不同的條件來看。香港是與世界溝通的良好橋樑，可以很好地保護知識產權，也很適合在海外推廣產品，這取決於你打算做的是什麼。也可能在中國大陸製造更為便宜，有時要將中國和香港的優勢有效結合，才能達到最佳的效果走向世界。

50. Are there internship opportunities for mentees?
會不會有實習的機會提供給學員呢？

Mentors try to help and guide mentees in their career development, which is beyond the scope of an internship. It is an opportunity for mentees to learn from the mentor in hope that they will be inspired to do better in the future. I did not have mentor/mentee programs in my days and I think it is one of the greatest things that we have now, where one can learn from someone who is more experienced. However, it is up to the mentee to demonstrate a willingness to learn through asking questions. At least you have the opportunity to do so. Treasure it.

導師要幫助和引導學生的職業生涯發展，這已經超越了實習機會。每一個學員有機會向導師學習，能激發起受教者去思想自己的未來。在我那個年代，我們沒有導師/學員計劃，我認為這是一個可以向更有經驗者學習的好機會。當然，這也是學生自己的意願，通過問問題來學習，至少你現在是有這樣的機會，好好珍惜它。

51. I understand that problems at work should be solved by myself when I become a senior, but if I really cannot solve the problem, how can I prove to others that even though I cannot solve the problem, I am still capable in my job?

我明白在工作上的問題應該由我自己解決，但如果我真的不能解決的情況下，我可以做些什麼向別人證明，即使我不能解決這個問題，我仍然有能力做好這份工作呢？

Sometimes, finding a solution may not be the solution. You can show others that you tried your best to resolve the problem and you do not give up in the process of trying. That may be good enough. If you try hard enough, you will always find a solution. Keep trying.

有些時候解決問題的辦法可能並不是簡單的找出解決方案，你可以向他人展示你努力地去尋找解決問題的過程，你不會放棄嘗試，這對你的同事來說可能就已經足夠了。如果你努力嘗試，你總會找出一個解決方案，繼續嘗試吧，這就是你需要展示的。

52. How can a normal person earn $1 million in a year by using normal methods?

一個普通人要怎樣通過正常的
途徑賺取一百萬年薪呢？

That is not difficult. If you are good in your field of work, you will be valued. If you can make $3 million for your employer, I'm sure he will pay you $1 million with ease. Many engineers make that kind of money if they are good at what they do and valuable to their employer.

這並不難，如果你在工作中很出色，你就會變得很有價值。如果你為你的僱主創造了每年三百萬的利潤，他會很容易地支付你每年一百萬的年薪，許多優秀的工程師也能做到，只要他們對僱主有價值便可以了。

53. Entrepreneurship has been a hot topic around the world, particularly among the young generation. Most young people love having the authority and freedom, while being able to explore which entrepreneurship can offer. Being an employee, while working on my own startup business, I learnt that entrepreneurship is more than just starting up your own business. Instead, I found that we should focus on the entrepreneurial spirit. Even employees (especially those who are highly educated) can have entrepreneurial spirit and this will be extremely helpful in their work. I would like to know how the entrepreneurial spirit could be fostered.

創業已經是世界上最熱門的話題，特別是在年輕一代。大部分年輕人希望得到創業家的權利，尊重和自由，同時還要能自我探索。作為一名僱員同時也是一名新的創業者，我覺得創業家精神不僅僅如此，不只是開啟自己的生意，而是要專注企業家精神。如果員工（特別是高學歷的）能有企業家精神，對其工作有非常大的幫助。我想知道企業家精神能不能被培養？

Entrepreneurship is a responsibility and it can also mean liability. Everyone wants to be their own boss but being a boss comes with responsibility to your staff, to the company, to make money, to sustain the business, to the society etc. One can always have entrepreneurial spirit with your own company or with a large corporation. One needs creativity and innovative skills in both. Your boss may value your innovative ideas. You can foster entrepreneurship through learning a broad spectrum of knowledge in management, marketing, accounting, and law. Not everyone is an entrepreneur; and risk taking is the key in entrepreneurship. Not everyone is willing to take or accept risk in our society.

創業同時也是有責任的，每個人都想自己做老板，但做老板必須對員工、公司、社會負責，要如何營利，如何持續發展生意等等。每間公司不論大小都可以好好利用企業家精神，企業家需要同時擁有創造和革新的能力，你的老板會欣賞你的創新想法。你能通過廣泛學習管理學累積經驗，通過學習市場推銷、會計學、法律等科目來培養你的企業家能量。不是每個人都能成為企業家，承擔風險是企業家最重要的一環，並不是每個人都願意承擔風險的。

54. What is the most difficult thing when starting a business?
開始一門生意最困難的地方是什麼？

Firstly, you will need to save enough capital for your business to survive. You will need to cover the carrying cost of the business. Secondly, marketing is also very important. You need to generate enough business to ensure the business is sustainable. You will need to have a good strategy before you start. You will also need to be conservative in your approach to ensure success.

首先你要有可以保持生意持續正常運營的啟動資金，支付營運成本。市場營銷也同樣重要，生意需要不斷發展才可持續下去。你還需要在開始前就有一個好的策略，要謹慎一點，這樣才有可能成功。

55. If do not know how to be firm with people, am I suited to be an Engineer or any other positions in the Engineering field?

如果我不懂得斥責別人，我適合做工程師的職位嗎？

There are many different approaches to motivate people to work for you. Being firm, or strict or even yelling are only some of the means to achieve certain objectives. You can be encouraging, instructive, demonstrative, negotiating, direct etc. You need to learn how to motivate different people in different ways. You have to learn how to achieve your objectives through different ways.

激勵他人為你工作有很多種方式，責罵只是實現某些目標的手段之一，還可以是友善鼓勵、協商、下指令等。你需要學習如何激勵其他人，不同的人需要不同的鼓勵方式，您要學習如何通過不同的方式來達到你的最終目標。

56. Shall we take up our favourite interest as a profession or just as a hobby?

我們應該把愛好當成職業還是僅僅作為一個興趣？

It can be both. If you are lucky to make your favourite interest or passion as a profession, you will enjoy it more.

If not, then do it as a hobby. You can also turn a hobby into a profession later in your life. In my case, mediation and arbitration were my interests and now I am more involved than other works. It occupies my time a lot more than my other profession. Priorities in your life will change as time goes by.

可以兩者結合的，如果你幸運的話可以將興趣當成職業，你會很享受。如果不行，就將興趣作為愛好吧。就我而言，調解和仲裁是我的興趣，但現在涉及在這兩方面的時間，甚至比我的專業更多。生活中的優先順序是會隨着時間改變的。

My Sharing
我的分享

Work can be both rewarding and satisfying. You must enjoy your work to have a happy life. You can always balance your work with other activities in your life. One needs to learn how to relax from the stresses of work. There are different skill sets that one can learn when managing others. Communication is the key ingredient to a harmonious work environment. Experience gained will benefit you in the long run. One needs to be flexible and ready for change. Adaptability will help you to blend into any work environment. Listen to your seniors as their experience can help you to progress in life. Work can be fun and enjoyable when you have a positive attitude towards work.

工作可以帶給人回報及成就感，學會如何享受工作會擁有更美好的人生。每個人都可以平衡工作與生活中的矛盾，要學會如何釋放工作上的壓力。同其他人相處，方式可以有很多種，經常與他人溝通是創造和諧工作環境的關鍵因素之一。豐富和充實的工作經驗會為你的長期事業發展提供一個很好的基礎，你要學會靈活地應對人生中各種的變化，良好的適應能力可以幫助您融入任何的工作環境。你應當經常聽取資深人士的意見，他們的經驗可以幫助你在人生中更加快速地進步。 只要你有積極進取的工作態度，工作就可以變得很愉快。

Career
職業

Everyone wants to create a better life for themselves. We all need to build our careers so we are able to fulfil all the needs in life. We all work hard and make progress in our careers so that we can earn more to improve our standard of living. One must not ignore the importance of one's career. It is your main source of income. So, the earlier you enter into the job market and make progress, the earlier that you can fulfill your needs in life.

職業可以為每個人的美好生活創造基礎，我們每個人都需要有良好的職業生涯來滿足我們的生活需求。我們要努力工作，在職業生涯中取得進展，才會獲得更大成就，提高生活水平。 我們不能忽視職業的重要性，因為這是收入的主要來源，你越早進入就業市場並越快進步，就能越快滿足到你生活上的需要。

Many will find getting that first job is most difficult. There always seems to be a scarcity of jobs available in the market. Yet, there are always opportunities. The real question is whether you are competent enough to take on the challenge in any new job. Your first job will largely depend on your level of education and holding a diploma will provide you with a better start than others. Work experience can also help you get a better job as it proves to the employer that you are competent and willing to work. Persistency in job hunting will get you your first job. Your first job may not bring you the most favourable economic return but if it provides you with the opportunity to learn, then it is the best job you can get.

許多人發現找第一份工作是最難的，總會覺得就業市場現有的機會不多。其實機會總是有的，問題是你是否有能力應付新工作的挑戰。你的第一份工作很大程度上取決於你的教育程度，你的文憑將是你最好的敲門磚，比他人有更好的開始。工作經驗可以幫助你更好地在工作上晉升，也向僱主證明你有能力也願意工作。畢業後找第一份工作是需要有耐心的，雖然它可能不一定會帶給你最好的經濟回報，但如果可以為你提供到好的學習機會，這便是你找到的最好的一份工作了。

One needs to be prepared and demonstrate willingness to work to any employer. One will always face obstacles in one's career. You will need to make changes and learn to resolve problems; and face many challenges throughout your career. I will highlight and share my experiences with you in hope that you will consider some of these important points below.

你要準備好並表明你是願意為僱主努力工作的，人在職業生涯中總有陷入困境的時候，你要隨時做出最快的變更，解決，和面對這些挑戰。我將會重點介紹一些這方面的觀點，並分享我的一些經驗，供各位考慮。

Questions & Answers
問題和答案

1. How can I present myself better in a job interview?
   如何在面試中脫穎而出？

   With good presentation and attitude, polite manners, a solid CV and strong handshake are necessary. Also, conduct proper research on the company that wants to hire you and try to find out more about the interviewer if you can. Be sincere and confident, maintain eye contact, and know the skills required for the job and point out what you can offer. Work will become your priority in life. Let them know you are prepared to work hard and convince the interviewer of the same.
   要有良好的表達能力和態度，要有禮貌，有完善的簡歷，事先對你要面試的公司做一些調研，或者了解一下面試你的人。誠懇的眼神接觸，強而有力的握手，要有自信，知道你可以或可能為這個公司帶來什麼，知道這個公司需要你的什麼技能。你願意努力工作，它將成為你人生中的首要重心，你要有這種說服力來面對你的面試官。

2. How best to prepare for a job interview?
   怎樣為面試做好準備？

   Create a solid CV and portfolio to highlight your strengths along with any work experience. Participation in student activities can highlight your leadership skills. Dress appropriately. Conducting research on the company is the best way to learn about what the company does and what they are looking for in a candidate. This will make you better prepared to answer any questions and to position yourself as the best candidate. When you know about the strengths and weaknesses of the company, you can identify areas that you can contribute to and make a good impression.

首先要有一份優秀的簡歷，強調你的優點及工作經驗，參與學生活動，展示你的領導能力，要有體面的衣着，對你要面試的公司和人士做好調研，了解這間公司的強與弱，確定你能幫公司帶來什麼。

3. Are there any career tips for a fresh graduate choosing his first job?

請問作為一名畢業生，在選擇第一份工作時，應注重哪些方面?

It is most important to know what you can learn from the company, and how stable and secure is the company in view of market or economic downturn. Getting started on your first job is better than having no job. Try to learn as much as you can during your term of employment.

你認為你能在這間公司裏學到什麼是最為重要的。其次是這間公司的經濟狀況如何，能否在市場下滑的時候安全渡過。無論如何，即使不是很喜歡也要先嘗試第一份工作，有好過無。不用太憂慮公司，而要考慮你在這職位期間能學到些什麼。

4. What is your view on the opportunities for an IT graduate?

請問你認為將讀完電信科的同學，畢業後的機遇如何？

You can explore opportunities both in Hong Kong and China. Shenzhen also provides many IT opportunities. Large or small companies provide different work experiences.

同時在香港和中國大陸探索機會，深圳也有很多電信行業的工作機會，大小公司都可能有不同的經驗。

5. Are there any self-help strategies and tips to improve one's mental and emotional health when one has difficulties facing challenges?

當面對挑戰時遇上挫折，應該如何調整自己的心理和情緒狀態？

Keep trying and stay positive. Obstacles can always be overcome if you don't give up and don't entertain negative thoughts. Focus on the bright side of everything and anything. One cannot fail if one keeps on trying. Also learn to seek guidance and advice from your seniors.

繼續嘗試並保持正面的態度，障礙一定是可以被克服的。不能放棄，不要只是想到負面而要想好的一面。只要繼續嘗試不可能永遠失敗的，也可以向你的長輩尋求意見及指引。

6. Most employers prefer fresh graduates from the Mainland to that of Hong Kong's. What about you?

很多僱主都很喜歡國內的畢業生而不是香港的，你呢？

I have no preference as long as the graduates are willing to work hard and learn. It will reflect on one's working attitude. Hong Kong students may be less exposed to temptations in life but this can change over time. That is why Hong Kong students need to learn how to operate both in China and Hong Kong. They must learn how to master the skills of communicating in Putonghua as a start.

我沒有對誰有偏好，只要這個畢業生是願意努力學習並努力工作的，這會很容易從他的工作態度反應出來。香港學生可能在某方面更能經受住誘惑的考驗，但這會很快改變過來，這也是為什麼香港學生也需要學會如何在香港或大陸工作，首先要從語言普通話開始。

7. As an employer, do you like a fresh graduate with a high GPA who has not participated in any activities at University or one with low GPA who has?

作為一名僱主，你會選擇一名高分數，但沒有參加過大學任何活動的畢業生，還是一名分數較低，但參加過很多學校活動的畢業生呢？

I will choose the one with a reasonable GPA and who has participated in University activities. Employers are not interested in those whom are active in political activities. A university student needs to focus on their studies and in areas of their interests in order to help them to grow in the right direction. A high GPA only proves that you can study but not necessarily show that you are an all-rounded individual. A low GPA might mean that you have not focused your energy on your studies and that you have over-extended yourself in other activities. The activities in which you participated are also important to an employer. They will look at the activities you were involved with and consider if they have made you a better person. Employers are not looking for someone who stands out from the crowd but rather, someone who can work for them in a productive manner.

我會選擇一名有中等分數並參加學校活動的學生，但不是搞政治活動的，學生需要關注那些能協助他增長學業和興趣的活動。高分數只代表你讀書不錯，但這不是全部。低分數意味着你並沒有全身心投入學習，並且可能太過於熱衷其他活動，這些活動涉及的范圍對僱主來說也很重要。他們會看這

些活動有沒有幫助你成為更優秀的人，你的僱主不是要一
名只懂得博出位的人，而是要一名能為他有效率地服務的僱
員。

8. What criteria you will consider when you hire a person?
   你聘請一個人時會考慮哪些條件？

The person must be willing to work hard and be willing to
learn and improve himself or herself. One must value one's
work and be devoted to work. One must be able to get
along with colleagues. One needs to be a team player and a
member of the team.
這個人是否願意努力工作，是否願意提升自己，他要珍惜他

的工作，必須要能和他的同事相處良好，能成為團隊的一份子。

9. When I asked the question today regarding the hiring of graduates, you mentioned a graduate needs to demonstrate that he or she is willing to work hard and learn during the interview. Apart from verbal skills, what other body language can I display to show that I have such abilities and leave a good impression?

今天我在詢問有關聘請畢業生時，閣下提到畢業生最重要的是在面試中表現出肯學肯拼的精神，請問除了用言語表達之外，我應該如何用不同的身體語言來給僱主一個正面和深刻的印象呢？

A strong handshake, maintain eye contact, sincerity in your voice and responses, and speak with confidence; these are important in order to make a good impression.

強而有力的握手，眼神接觸，誠懇的態度，自信的談吐，這些都是能讓你給僱主一個正面深刻印象的重要元素。

10. How do I find a job? It seems very difficult.

找工作似乎很難，應該怎麼辦？

It is difficult to find your first job in any economy or country. The only advice I can give you is keep trying. Send out as many resumes as possible. Before I got an interview for my first job in Canada, I sent out over 200 letters to potential employers. Prepare for the interview. You need to get to know the company prior going into the interview. You need to know what they expect from you. It is best to work on any job rather than not working at all. Your future employer will at least appreciate that you are a hard worker rather than doing nothing at all with your time. Your willingness and enthusiasm towards work plays an important factor to any potential employer who is considering you for the job.

不論在哪個國家哪個行業想要得到第一份工都是很難的，你唯一能做的是努力不斷嘗試，發送簡歷出去越多越好。我以

前在加拿大時，就是發送了超過200封簡歷，之後才獲得一次面試。你也要為面試做好準備，面試前應該要多了解這間公司，估計他們對你的期望。不論是什麼工作總比完全沒有工作要好，你將來的老闆會欣賞你對工作的熱衷而不是無所事事，你對工作的熱誠會是對你將來的僱主在考慮中的一個很重要的因素。

11. How do you find a high-paying part-time job? My current job is relatively low-paying.

怎樣可以找到一份高薪的兼職工作？我目前的工作相對來講人工比較低。

Part-time work will never be high-paying. Employers want you to be committed to your job. Having a job is better than not having one. You can gain experience through working and hopefully some day you can get a higher paying job. Learn what you can in your present job.

兼職是永遠不可能高薪的。僱主希望你能全身投入,有一份工作總比沒有的好。你可以通過工作獲得經驗,希望有一天你可以獲得一份更高工資的工作,但首先要在現有的工作中好好學習。

12. You mentioned that if one walks out of one's comfort zone, one would gain more in life. What do I need prepare before I walk out of my comfort zone? Do I need to be financially stable? I worry if I walk out of my comfort zone unprepared, I will fail.

請問走出舒適圈前需要準備甚麼呢?根據您於聚餐時所說,您多次強調如果想得到更多,便要走出舒適圈,不要甘於過着平淡無奇的生活。請問走出舒適圈前需要做哪些準備呢?是否需要先有穩定的財政狀況?我明白 "不入虎穴,焉得虎子" 的道理,但我擔心如果沒有甚麼準備,便走出舒適圈冒險,恐怕會失敗。

Firstly, you need to be financially capable. That means you do not quit your job until you have a new one. You need to know your objectives in any change to your career or job. Is it about moving ahead, learning different skills or because you dislike your present boss? There is no guarantee that you will like your next or future boss. Calculate the risks involved, as you need to evaluate if you can afford these risks before you proceed. You also need to know what you will gain, as a reason for moving away from your comfort zone. Your age will have an impact upon your decision. Your "liabilities" in life such as your family, your children, your mortgage etc. will influence your ultimate decision.

首先，你要確保自己有經濟承受能力。如果你要辭職，要先找到工作才請辭。在辭職的時候，應該要知道自己的目標，是為以後可以更加進步，可以學習到不同的技能，還是因為不喜歡你現有的老板？將來的老板也沒有人可以保證你一定會喜歡，這些都是一些存在的風險。你需要評估你自己是否能夠承擔這些風險，你要明白到你從舒適圈裏出來之後，會得到什麼。通常你的年齡會影響你的決定，你在人生中的責任，比如對家庭，孩子，房屋按揭等，都會影響你作出最終決定。

13. How can I prepare myself for my future career?
    怎樣為我將來的事業做好準備？

Learn everything and anything. You will not know when you will need a particular skill. Focus on the areas that you are working on. You need to be an expert in all related disciplines of your work.

學習所有和全面的東西，你不知道什麼時候真正需要那種特別的

技能。主要先去關注你工作領域方面的知識，你需要成為工作領域中各方面的專家。

14. Is work experience or talent more important?
    是工作經驗重要還是才能更為重要？

Work experience is vital. Many people have certain talents or abilities. One could gain abilities through different work experiences. One must work hard to learn and gain abilities but work experience requires chance and opportunities.

工作經驗是至關重要的，很多人都有一定的才能，但不同的工作經驗可以使你得到不同的才能。每個人都可以通過努力工作而獲得不同的才能，但工作經驗是需要機遇和命運安排的。

15. Peer pressure
    同輩的壓力

Choosing between the loves of friends or following one's life goals is something that many people face in life. Yet, many people choose to be loved by a group of friends instead of pursing one's goal. How could we improve this by balancing between peer pressure and following own goals?

在朋友和人生目標之中做出選擇，這是很多年輕人會面對的問題，很多人選擇了朋友，我們應該怎麼平衡同輩壓力和我們自己的人生目標呢？

You can always make many friends or belong to different groups of friends in life. You can also pursue your life goals and make friends. One does not need to stick with one set of friends for life. You have to achieve different objectives at different stages of your life. Your friends will not necessarily help you to achieve this. If you are successful, you will be loved by many friends and if you fail, not many of them will still be around. Do not worry about friends. Some friends will appreciate you more than others. One always needs to trust oneself and try to achieve one's own goals instead of worrying about others' views.

人的一生可以交很多不同的朋友或朋友的圈子，你可以同時追逐夢想和交不同的朋友。一個人不應該僅限於一個圈子內的朋友，人的一生應該在不同時候有不同的追求，朋友不一定會幫助你完成夢想，如果你成功了，你會有很多朋友，但如果你失敗了，又有多少人在你的身邊呢？不用擔心朋友，總有些朋友會比其他人更欣賞你。只要你相信自己， 努力達成自己的夢想，而不要去擔心別人對你的看法。

16. After studying in Hong Kong for a year, I discovered that Hong Kong has a highly efficient working environment. How does a Hong Kong person relax himself to release his work pressure in their non-working hours?

我在香港學習了一年多，發現香港有很高效率的工作環境，除了工作外，香港人怎樣去放鬆自己，怎樣釋放工作壓力？

Exercise is a good way to relax; whereas some people choose reading or going on holidays or meeting with friends to expand their social network. There are many things that need to be done each day and it is best not to leave it to tomorrow since there is always something new tomorrow that needs to be done. Accomplishment can be a big driving force in life. When you accomplish a task, it gives you satisfaction and releases your work pressure as well.

運動是很好的放鬆良藥，有的人選擇看書、行山、渡假、朋友聚會，擴大自己的社交網絡。每天都有很多東西需要做，最好不要把它留到明天，因為明天總有一些新的東西要做。成就感可以是人生的一大驅動力，當一個人能達成一定的目標，這會帶來一定的滿足感，也會讓你將壓力釋放出去的。

17. I am 22 now and still very young to decide my lifetime career, but I don't think being an environmental consultant is what I want. At the same time, I worked so hard to study the knowledge in this field and I don't want to waste it. Is there any job that you know of where I can incorporate my knowledge to become a professional such as an environmental lawyer or an environmental mediator/arbitrator?

我現在22歲，我想現在來決定我一生的職業還是太年輕，但我不認為環境顧問將是我未來一生的職業。同時，我還在努力學習這個領域的知識，因為我不想浪費已學的知識。有哪種職業，可以將我已學的環境學科的知識轉換成為專業，如環境律師或環境調解員/仲裁員？

I wish I was 22 again! From what I can gather from your question, I think you can first be an engineer and then study law to become a lawyer. You can study a part-time Bachelor of Laws. I think there is one at HKU. It will be hard work.

I did half of that degree in my younger days. Consider it carefully and meanwhile, check out HKIE's requirements in getting yourself qualified as an engineer. What you have learnt will not go to waste. Once you become an engineer, people will recognize you as a specialised professional in the environmental discipline and in addition you can also choose to be a lawyer. It will definitely add value to your credentials as a professional.

我也希望我是22歲，哈哈。通過你提出的問題來分析，我覺得你可以先做工程師然後考慮做法律行業。你可以去兼讀一個法律學士課程，香港大學有這樣的課程，但這會十分艱苦。我年輕的時候也讀了半個這課程，你可以先去了解一下。同時，調查一下香港工程師學會要如何成為一名環境工程師資格的要求，以便你所學的不會造成浪費，一旦你成為一名環境工程師，他人已知你在環境領域上的專才。如果同時可以成為一名律師，這將會對你在專業人士身份上增加一定的份量。

18. Although I have worked for a year and a half in this company now, I am still not sure if I want to stay in this field for the rest of my life. I always want to explore more fields of work or explore the world when I am still young. However, I am not sure how to do it. Could you give me some advice on this matter?

雖然我在這間公司已工作了一年半，我仍然不確定是否一輩子會做這個行業，我總想趁我還年輕的時候，擴展我的工作範圍或者去探索一下這世界，然而我不確定應該如何做，你能給我一些建議嗎？

It is important to get your qualification first before you change fields. If you are qualified in one profession, you always have the choice to go back on your decisions. You can always explore other job opportunities. You can travel and see more of the world. Once you join HKIE, there are different seminars that you can join and see where your interests take you. You could join seminars of different disciplines that are organised regularly. I am sure you will find what you want to do in due course. In the meantime, learn and understand what you can in your present job.

在你做出改變之前，很重要的一點是你要先拿到第一個基本資格。當你有了第一個基本資格後，你才可以有機會選擇走回頭路。你也可以探討其它的工作機會，或者旅遊走遍世界。如果你加入了工程師學會，你可以去參加不同的研討會，可以啟發你究竟對哪方面更感興趣，他們定期有不同的學術研討會可以讓你參加。我覺得這樣你一定會找到你想要的方向。現時來說，你要從現在的工作中加以學習和了解。

19. Did you pick your career path based on your interests or what you were good at? Or was it for other reasons?
在你的職業規劃中，你是選擇興趣還是你最擅長的？還是其它因素？

I picked my career because my family was involved in construction and property. At the start of my career, I thought of nothing else but construction. It was not until later in my career, in 1999, that I was involved in other sectors like telecommunication networks. It was not a matter of choice but of needs. Being involved in telecommunication meant I had an urgent need to learn about it and that's when I got myself directly involved in that sector. I also got involved in arbitration and mediation. This was more of an interest initially and it has gradually developed into a career. I just happen to be involved in different careers at different times. I always try to make the best of any career that I am involved with at any given time.

我選擇建築行業是因為我的家族是做房地產及建築的。所以在我一開始，我只想到做建築行業，直到後期我才有所改變。在1999年，我進入另一領域——電信網絡，這其實不是一個選擇，而是必需。我們投資了電信網絡，所以我急需要了解和認知這個行業。接着我又同時進入了調解和仲裁行業，這本來是我興趣之一，然而後期又變成事業的一部份。我也是很偶然地在不同的時段進入了不同的行業，但我不論甚麼時段，我都會盡力在每一行業做得最好。

20. I found some information on the internet about mediation and arbitration when I was studying this course. I found that there are some environmental dispute issues that might need a mediator or arbitrator with some knowledge in the environmental discipline. Do you know any mediators or arbitrators of this kind? If yes, could you share their career experience with me? What should I do to become one of them?

我在學習本課程時，在互聯網上找到了一些關於調解和仲裁的信息，我發現有一些環境糾紛問題，可能需要一個仲裁員或調解員能在環境科上有一定的知識。你知道這類型的調解員或仲裁員嗎？如果有，你能分享他的職業經歷嗎？如果我想成為其中的一員，我該怎麼辦？

Many mediators or arbitrators with a civil engineering background can do mediation or arbitration in the environmental discipline. If you become an environmental lawyer, you can also become an environmental mediator or arbitrator. Experience is more important for mediation and arbitration practices. You do need some knowledge in law to be a good mediator or arbitrator. There are international mediators and arbitrators who specialise in these areas but I do not think there are any in Hong Kong at present. I do read and study a lot of material on arbitration, mediation, and the law throughout my arbitration and mediation career. It takes years of practical experience to become a good arbitrator and mediator.

許多具有土木工程背景的調解員或仲裁員，都可以在環境領域中進行調解和仲裁。如果你成為一名環境律師，你也可以成為環境調解員或仲裁員。在調解和仲裁方面的經驗更為重要，你需要一些法律知識才能成為一個好的調解員和仲裁員。在海外有國際調解員和仲裁員專門從事這方面的工作，但到現在為止香港還沒有專門做這方面的調解員和仲裁員。我本人在仲裁和調解事業過程中，需要閱讀和研究很多仲裁，調解和法律方面相關的資料，需要多年的工作經驗才能成為一名好的仲裁員和調解員。

My Sharing
我的分享

Many obstacles can be overcome with a consistent and persistent attitude. One's career is an important part of a person's life. Most people spend over 8 hours a day working to excel in their careers. We all hope to start our career with a high-paying salary and rewarding work or even become the boss. Not all of us may be able to satisfy such a wish but we can always achieve this through hard work and making positive changes.

很多困難都可以通過堅持不懈的努力來解決。職業生涯是人生中最重要的組成部分，大部分人的工作時間大大超過每天8小時，才能在職業生涯中脫穎而出。每個人都希望從事高薪而有意義的工作或自己做老板，但不是每個人都能滿足到這樣的願望，只有通過努力工作才可能實現這一願望。

Action will speak for itself. One must put oneself into action. Begin with less rather than not begin at all. One needs to work rather than not work at all. One can explore different areas to seek one's ultimate destiny. Your job should not stop you to explore other areas of interest. Interests can also become part of your career.

行動本身就是一種語言，一定要讓自己付諸行動。一個人要從基礎做起，開始總比不開始好。每個人都可以探索不同領域來尋求自己的最終目標。你現有的工作不會妨礙你去探索其他感興趣的領域，興趣也可能將來成為你職業生涯的一部份。

One may need to walk out of one's comfort zone from time to time in order to excel. Progression will come with risks. You must calculate the risks involved before making any changes and assess yourself to see whether you are prepared to take the risk or not. You need to work hard to create a good foundation in your career. This can help you to achieve your dreams more realistically. Basic training and enhanced learning improves your knowledge to allow you to be prepared for future challenges. Building a career is always hard work but you will enjoy the reward that comes with a good career.

一個人可能需要走出你的舒適圈，才能超越現狀。當然進展也同時帶來一定的風險和挑戰，所以在做任何改變之前，先要計算好當中的風險，你是否能承擔。努力能為你的職業生涯打造一個良好基礎，可以幫助你更容易實現你的夢想。基礎培訓和持續進修可以提升你的認知能力，使你對未來的挑戰作好準備。做好一份職業是艱辛的，但如果你擁有一份好的職業，就可以享受到它帶來的美好成果。

點
解

Investment
投資

Investment helps you to create wealth. It helps you to multiply your money. Wealth can improve your standard of living. You can then satisfy your needs in life and accumulate savings for those rainy days. Many people may know how to make money but they do not know how to invest or they invest poorly. Surprisingly, this applies to many highly educated individuals.

投資能幫你創造財富，提高生活水平，它可以幫你用錢賺錢。你可以因而滿足人生需求，並為將來積累儲蓄。許多人可能只懂得如何賺錢，但他們不懂如何投資或常常做出錯誤的投資。最驚人的是，這點常適用於許多受過高等教育的人士。

If improper investment is made, inflation will depreciate your money. Most investments are risky. Therefore, you need to know your limits in any investment. One shall not invest beyond your own means. "The higher the risk means the higher the return." One also needs to be objective when making investments. Word of mouth or recommendations from friends is usually the beginning of a mistake.

如果投資不當，通貨膨脹會使你的錢貶值。大多數的投資都有一定的風險，因此，您需要了解你自己的投資上限，不能超出自己的能力範圍去投資，風險越高，回報越高。做投資時也需要客觀分析，傳言或朋友推薦通常是投資錯誤的開始。

In addition, one must not over borrow. Borrowing often results in over investment. One shall always be conservative and maintain slow growth in your investment. Do not look for short-term gains but always take a long-term perspective in your investment. Invest in products that you can maintain and manage. Be careful with your investments, as they will often bring surprises in life and even a better life for you and your family. I will share some of my insights on investments in this section of the book.

另外一點是不能過度借貸，借款會使你容易過度投資。投資一定要保守謹慎，保持循序漸進，不要只尋找短期收益，應該從長遠角度來看待投資。要投資可持續和容易管理的產品，謹慎投資往往會為你的人生帶來驚喜，也為你和家人帶來更美好的明天。在本節中，我將與你分享我對投資的一些見解。

Questions & Answers
問題與答案:

Money Matters
金錢問題

1. There is no doubt that we need to properly manage our own cash flow. Yet just saving money in the bank is not sufficient. Can you give me some advice on how to use my money wisely on investments?
    毫無疑問管理好自己的現金流是很重要的，然而，將錢存放在銀行是不劃算的，你可否給我一些建議，如何適當地用現金投資？

You will need to save your first pot of gold to form basic capital for investment. You will not be able to make money from the bank. The bank will always win. There are too many experts working for the bank who help minimize their risks. You can only make money from hard work and saving. You will need to invest in some value-adding or appreciating items/industries with growth potential e.g. real estate, property, land, education etc., and you should not invest in some depreciating consumer goods e.g. cars, cameras, watches, etc.

你需要首先儲存第一筆錢作為你投資的基本資本，你不可能從銀行賺到錢，銀行永遠是贏家，他們有太多的專家在為他們工作，減少自身的風險。你只能通過努力工作來儲錢，要投資一些有增值潛力的東西/行業，比如不動產和自身增值的東西等等，而不應買一些會貶值的消費品上，比如汽車、照相機、手錶等。

2. How do you manage your assets?

你是怎樣管理好你的資產？

You need to get involved in the details of all your financial matters. You have to know how to control your investments. You need to have a "hands on" approach in order to have control over managing your assets. Do not expect others to fulfill all your needs. Follow up on delegated tasks personally. Set up a system. Remember tasks that have not been completed and try to complete them as soon as possible. Do not miss deadlines; and do not neglect issues that have not been addressed yet.

你首先要知道你的資產投資的全部內容，自己親自管理所有細節，力不到不為財，不要指望別人能滿足你所有的要求。跟進你的資產所有要做的事項，設立一個跟進系統，以便記住那些還沒有完成的事情可盡快完成。不要錯過最終期限，不能有任何遺漏未完成的事項。

3. If one wants a better standard of living in Hong Kong, it is essential for one to be involved with investment. So how can I develop an investment strategy that best fits my needs? 現今的香港，如果想獲得更充裕的生活水平，投資是必不可缺的，請問如何更好建立自己的投資眼光？

Investment is important yet saving for your first pot of gold is more important. If you do not have your first pot of gold, it will be impossible for you to invest. Knowledge is the key to success in investment. You need to know the economics of the society, the potential growth areas in the society, the trends of the market; and learn to develop your own evaluation and intuition on the future and potential growth areas before you invest. So start saving early and learn general knowledge on investing. The earlier you save, the sooner you can start investing.

投資是很重要但更為重要的是要先擁有你的第一桶金，如果你沒有第一筆資金，你不可能去做任何投資。知識是投資成功的關鍵，你需要知道這個社會的經濟走向情況，社會中有發展潛力的領域，市場的趨勢，在投資之前對有投資潛力的領域進行分析。現在第一步先開始儲錢和學習常識，越早開始儲錢你就越早可以開始投資。

4. How can I be successful if I lack the resources such as money and connections? 缺乏資源的時候（如金錢，關係），我如何能取得成功？

You cannot invest if you have no money, only saving can help you. Connections and relationships are meaningless. It is a misconception. Connections cost money and it may not help you during critical times. It is knowledge that will ensure progress in your career. Continuous learning will properly equip you when opportunities arise.

沒有錢是做不了投資的，只有儲錢才能幫助你。關係並不重要的，這是一個錯覺。關係不是免費的，而且也不一定在危急的時候能幫到你。只有學識而不是關係才能幫到你的事業發展，持續學習能讓你裝備好自己面對機會的來臨。

5. If I am going to invest for the future, what should I invest in?
   如果我想投資未來，我應該投資什麼？

Real Estate and Education are what you should invest in. All of the tycoons in the world are somehow involved with real estate and property. It is one of the most secure revenue investments. You can start out small and grow from it. You can then leverage from your investments. However, you have to make sure you can bear the burden of debt when the market is down; otherwise you will lose all of your investments. As for education, you are actually investing in knowledge and yourself to prepare for future challenges.

房地產和教育知識是最好的投資，世界上所有的大富翁都涉足於房地產，這些資產擁有最安全的收入。你可以從小的投資開始，你也可以利用槓桿來進行投資。然而，你還是要確保自己可以承擔市場下滑時產生的負債，否則你會損失掉所有你的投資。至於投資於教育知識，你其實是投資給自己以準備應付未來的挑戰。

6. How can I buy a flat if I'm not a doctor, engineer, businessman or a professional?
如果我不是一名醫生、工程師、商人或專業人士，我怎樣可能買到一層樓呢？

Surely, there are many different professionals who are able to buy a flat. A chef can buy a flat; a steel worker can buy multiple flats. If you are the best in your field of trade/profession and you don't spend beyond your means, you can save enough to buy your flat. Start small and buy bigger only when you can afford it. We all start small and work our way to improve in our life.
當然，還有很多不同行業的人都可以買樓。一個廚師可以買一個單位，一個做鋼筋的工人也可以買到多個單位。如果你在你的專業領域中是最好的，而且開銷有度，在正常情況下你是可以節省到足夠來買你的住所的。開始時可以是小小的，慢慢改善，一定要是你能負擔得起的。我們都是從小的單位開始，慢慢改善我們的生活的。

7. What is the best sustainable business strategy that is easily implemented, e.g. sustainable eco-building materials that can substitute traditional materials?
有哪種生意策略是實際上容易操作的，像一些可持續的生態建築材料可以代替傳統材料嗎？

There is no simple and easy way to do business. Every business takes hard work to set up and maintain. Sustainable eco-building materials require support from the government and policy-makers before it can be profitable since sustainable materials tend to be more expensive than traditional materials. Recycling costs money. Even though it is environmentally friendly, it will cost more. So governments need to support this kind of initiative before private sectors will follow.

做生意沒有簡單和容易的方式,每一門生意都需要努力來開發和持續下去。生態建築材料需要政府的政策支持才可成功,因為通常生態建築材料會比傳統材料更昂貴,回收材料是有代價的,但對環境保護有利。政府的支持是先決條件,然後私人企業才會跟進。

點
解

My Sharing
我的分享

Investment is important to the growth of your assets. You need to invest to create a better future for you and your family. However, one shall not over investment or over borrow. Growth needs to be progressive. There are no quick dollars in life.

One needs to work hard and it requires time to accumulate wealth and growth. One shall start small and grow progressively. Many lack the resources to invest but saving and discipline will help you to accumulate enough wealth for investing. It is never too late to start so start saving today and invest for tomorrow.

投資對你的資產增長極為重要，你需要投資來為你和你的家人創造更美好的未來。但是切不可過度投資或過度借貸，投資增長需要逐步漸進，不要相信有一夜暴富的神話。你需要努力工作和時間累積儲蓄及財富增長，從小的開始，逐漸增長。許多人開始時缺乏投資的資金基礎，這必須通過儲蓄和有規律的生活來積累足夠的資金，以用於投資。從今天開始儲蓄吧，永遠不會太遲的，投資於未來。

Family
家庭

Family is a safe haven or sanctuary for everyone. This is where you can rest, recharge and prepare for your next challenge. There is often conflict that might arise between family members, husband and wife or between a parent and their child. Such conflicts are mostly based on good intentions. However, miscommunication often causes good intentions to turn bad. One needs to learn how to appreciate family members and their intentions to be able to "read between the lines". Different people will express their views differently. We must appreciate family members who behave or act out of good intentions.

家庭是每個人的庇護所，是你可以休息，充電和迎接下一個挑戰的地方。 父母與子女之間，家庭成員之間，丈夫與妻子之間經常會發生許多衝突，這些衝突往往是基於良好的意願，但因為溝通不合當而引致好事變壞事。我們要學習如何欣賞家人的思維，並在言語之間讀出他們的意願。不同的人用不同的表達方式來表達自己，我們必須欣賞家人的行為是出於良好初衷的。

Parents often impose pressure upon their child and hope that they will do better and be more competitive in their life. They often want their child to be a decathlon gold medalist; an expert or genius of knowledge; a superhuman athlete, and have a reputable professional career. They want him or her to be top of their class at school in all subjects and disciplines, or show outstanding achievement and conduct as well. Some of these expectations are unrealistic and almost impossible to achieve. Such pressure leaves the child very little time for normal growth and enjoyment in his or her childhood life. Parents sometimes even want their child to achieve what they did not or could not achieve in their own lifetime.

父母經常對孩子施加壓力，希望他們能做得更好，在人生中更有競爭力。有時甚至希望他們的孩子成為十項全能的金牌得主、萬事通、超人，以後更要有一份良好的專業。他們希望孩子在學校裏不論是體育，還是音樂，或是在所有學科中都能表現出類拔萃。但這當中很多期望是不切實際的，或是不可能實現的任務。這些壓力讓孩子全沒有時間過一個正常而享受的年輕人生活。家長有時甚至希望孩子實現他們以前未能達到的人生目標。

As a youngster, one tries to satisfy the needs of his or her parents and follows the social norm. This behaviour often leaves little opportunity for the youngster to grow in his or her own way. One will feel frustrated in the lack of freedom and from the constant bombardment of schoolwork and extra curricular activities. There is no time for relaxation and play. The youngster becomes overwhelmed and depressed and they can not share this problem with their parents or siblings either.

年輕人總會試圖滿足父母的需要，符合社會行為的規範。 對於年輕人來說，以他自己的方式成長的機會變得很少。他在生活中缺乏自主權，受到學校功課和多項額外課程的不斷轟炸而感到十分沮喪，沒有時間放鬆和玩樂，而父母及兄弟姐妹卻無法與他分擔苦惱。

As we grow older, we will begin to understand and appreciate the good intentions of our parents. However, there are often other problems that will arise in life as we begin to worry about how to find a balance between our family and work, or what we can do for our parents in return; and how does one establish a future family of our own, or when is the right time to start our own family, etc. These are all important decisions in one's life. One needs to understand the basis for these issues before making any final decisions. I hope I can shed some light on some of these concerns.

隨着年齡的增長，我們開始懂得感激父母的良好意願，但是其他問題也會接踵而來，我們開始擔心如何在家庭和工作之間取得平衡，我們可以為父母做些什麼，如何建立我們自己的家庭，什麼時候開始自己的家庭生活等等。人生中有很多重要時刻，在作出最終決定之前，必須要了解這些問題的基本元素，我希望通過我的分享可以幫助你解答一些你所關注的問題。

Questions & Answers:
問題與答案

1. Parents and Children
   父母與子女

   When one is faced with dream or reality, why do people usually give up on chasing their dreams? Why is it so hard to get approval from family? Family should be supportive and understanding towards each other. However, in many cases, I have seen parents cruelly destroying the dreams of young people by cutting off their wings to stop them chasing their dreams. Our paths should be determined by ourselves, but parents often like to use the reason "it's for your own good...", so do we follow our dreams or only live in reality?

   在夢想和現實生活之間，為什麼很多人總是選擇放棄追求夢想？而且很難得到家人的支持？家人應該是互相支持和理解對方的，但是很多時候，我見到家長們總是折斷青年人的夢想。我們的人生應該是由自己決定，但父母總喜歡什麼都幫我們作出決定，還總是說 "為你好……"。我們是應該跟隨自己的夢想還是接受現實呢？

When chasing dreams, we need to be realistic about it and it needs to work within our own abilities. It would be silly or foolish if one tries to go beyond one's ability. You are an adult and you should make your own decisions. Parents can only guide you and you make your own decisions for your own future, regardless whether they are good or bad. You will need to bare the consequences of the path you choose. Parents always try to give their best judgement in life based on their experiences. They don't mean any harm to you in any way, so the least you can do is to listen to them and evaluate the situation based on their recommendations and decide for yourself. You will need to live and bear the consequences of your decisions, not them. Parents will always think "it's for your own good…", so at least consider their views before making any decision as there's no harm in listening anyway.

追求夢想的同時不可以不切實際，我們要在能力範圍之內做事。當有些人想要超越自己的能力做不可能做到的事情，這只是在異想天開。你是一個成年人，也應該要自己決定自己的命運，父母只能指引你，但最終還是你自己來決定你的將來。不論這個結果是好是壞，你總是要承擔最終後果。父母總是會用他們的人生經驗給你最好的意見，任何時候他們都不會傷害你，所以最起碼的，你應該要學會如何聆聽他們的意見，然後根據他們的意見來重新審視你的決定。你的人生道路是一系列的選擇和決定，而決定權在於你自己，不是他們。父母總是想"為你好……"，所以在你下決定之前，多考慮一下他們的意見，這總是沒有壞處的。

2. Why must girls get married before 30 years old? Or she will be labelled as a "spinster"! This is totally stressful for women who are close to the age of 30. So how is it fair that men can get married at any age without being labelled?

女孩子必須在30歲以前結婚嗎？否則就會被貼上"剩女"的標籤？這會讓每個臨近30歲的女孩子有很大的心理壓力。而男人便可以在任何時候結婚卻不會被貼標籤，這樣公平嗎？

I disagree with labeling. I did not marry my wife until she was 42. She had a satisfying and tough career and she worked hard to achieve it without thinking about marriage. What others think is not important. It is important that you decide your own destiny. Marriage is a lifelong commitment and it is best to marry someone who is your friend; and someone who you can share and spend the rest of your life with, rather than marry for the sake of marriage or because of others' views. Others do not live your life, you do. Focus on your work and create your own future.

我不同意標籤化。我和我太太結婚的時候，她已經42歲，她有一份很優秀也很豐富的履歷，一直以來她所考慮的都是努力工作而不是婚姻。其它人怎樣想並不重要，你自己怎樣決定你的命運才最重要。一段婚姻是終生的，想要能維持一生這麼長的時間，最好是找一個你可以做朋友的伴侶，可以分享並且共度下半生的人，而不是考慮到因為要結婚而結婚或因別人的想法來結婚。他人並不能代替你來決定你的人生，關注你的工作並創造你自己美好的未來。

3. Can women have the same work prospects and opportunities as men when living in a big city? If not, why?
作為女性在大城市打拼會不會和男孩子有一樣好的前景？如果沒有，為什麼？

Hong Kong is a diverse and vibrant city that provides its people with prosperity and freedoms, as well as gender equality for both men and women. At times, women can have more advantages over men. There are many leaders in the community who are women, in both Hong Kong and China. The most important thing is that you have the knowledge you need for your work or the industry. One can always do well and make it in the industry or workplace if you are the best. For example, in the construction industry, onsite conditions are tough and sometimes women find it uncomfortable so they move to other positions within the industry like consultancy. Yet there are many good project managers and engineers in the construction industry in which all of whom are women.

香港對男性女性來講都是很公平的，有些時候女性還更有優勢。你可以看到香港和中國國內很多團體，公司及官場的領導者都是女性。最重要的是你自己是否擁有在行業需要的學識，如果你擁有足夠優秀學識，定能脫穎而出。在建築行業，工地環境是比較艱苦的，有時女性會覺得不方便，所以會轉移到其它崗位如顧問公司等工作。但在這行業也有很多好的項目經理及工程師是女性。

4. What are the factors, do you think if any, are restricting the development of women in the workplace?
   在職場中，有些什麼因素會限制女性的發展？

   I do not see any restrictions at all. The only restriction is you. You have to overcome and embrace the fact that men generally dominate the construction industry yet they will also treat their female counterparts and coworkers as brothers. I recall that during work onsite, we used to all go out and have lunch or dinner together and play mahjong.
   我覺得這方面是完全沒有限制的，唯一的限制在於你自己。你必須要適應和接受現在的建築行業普遍由男性主導，我們同樣會視女性員工為兄弟一樣，我記得以前我在工地的時候，很多時大家都會一起外出吃飯或者打麻將。

5. Has the status quo for women improved compared to 10 years ago?
   現在女性的地位比起十年前有提高嗎？

   There are currently more women engineers and senior executives when compared to 10 years ago. The construction industry seems to accept roles for women in engineering who also work in contracting, consultancy, and teaching positions. Women are also in senior positions of many corporations, political organisations, governments and non-profit organisations. So I believe that the status quo for women in Hong Kong will make leaps and bounds in the forseeable future.

比起十年前，現在有更多的女工程師和女性在各領導班子。
在建築行業，似乎已更接受女工程師在施工、顧問或教學等
方面的職位。很多女性也在不同的大公司、官場、政府和其
他自願團體身居高職，我相信女性在香港的地位是沒有止境
的。

6. My only siblings are twin sisters from my stepfather's family
    and one of my dreams is help them follow their own life
    goals. A lot of our family relatives love to compare me to my
    sisters, and to be honest I do not like that at all. I don't want
    them to follow my footsteps and bear the pressure from their
    peers. I want them to live out their own dreams, because
    it's their life - not mine and certainly not my relatives either.
    Do you have any suggestions as to what I can do for my
    sisters? Also, as the only man in the house, since we were
    kids I had to take up the role of a son, a brother and a
    "shadow husband"; and I am wondering what more can I do
    so that every single member of my family can live with their
    own life.

    我有兩個孿生姐妹（同母異父），我的夢想是希望她們能找
    到她們自己的人生目標。很多親戚喜歡拿我的姐妹和我作比
    較，但其實我並不喜歡。我不希望他們跟隨着我的足跡，承
    受來自朋輩的壓力，我希望她們能有自己的夢想和目標。因
    為無論如何，談到生命，那是她們自己的人生，不是我的，
    也不是那些親戚的。我可以為她們提出些什麼建議呢？我
    是家裏唯一的男孩子，所以從小開始，我就扮演着家中的兒
    子，兄弟和隱形丈夫。我在想有什麼辦法可以讓我的家人不
    要再依靠我，而能有他們自己的生活。

If your sisters can afford to live their life goals, that will be great. They can then go into a profession of their choice. But not everyone can be that lucky. Your relatives may think that you have been doing well and that is why they want your sisters to follow your footsteps but the question is – do they want to do it or not? If so, it is fine. If not, then you have to evaluate and analyse with them what they want to do in life and try to help them to achieve as much as possible. Just enjoy whatever you do; and life will take its course. I suggest that you must communicate with your sisters and see what makes them happy and what they have in mind for their life. Always understand the situation before taking further action. This is what we learn in engineering. Each member of your family will live their own life. So more importantly for you now is that firstly, you must live a good life. Only when you are free from worries, then you can take care and look out for your sisters and family.

如果你的姐妹們可以有他們自己的目標，這當然最好，他們可以選擇進入自己的專業道路。但是並不是每個人都那麼幸運的，你的親戚可能認為你做得很好，所以他們也希望你的姐妹們可以跟隨你的腳步，但問題的關鍵在於他們自己想不想走這條路。如果想的話當然好，但如果不想，你應該要幫她們評估一下她們適合做些什麼，並且盡可能地幫助她們，實現她們的夢想。享受你現在所做的，命運自會有安排。我建議你首先要與你的姐妹們溝通，看看他們覺得有樂趣的是什麼。行動前要先了解實況，這是我們在工程學中學到的。他們會有自己的生活。現在最重要的是你首先要能有一個好的生活，如果你自己的生活都有很多顧慮，你不可能再去照顧他們。

7. If there is conflict between my work and family, what should I do?

如果事業和家庭互相有冲突，應該做出怎樣的決擇？

Your family will understand you. They will always support you no matter what the circumstances. Your family is your shelter for when you face difficulties. I am sure that your family will not stop you from progressing in your career. However, there is often conflict that arises when parents want their children to be around yet work requires them to be elsewhere. Family wants to remain close to you but sometimes work may not allow that to happen. Family members or parents often want their children to

be independent but at the same time still want them to be nearby. Eventually they understand that sooner or later, children will grow up and will be independent. You will have to determine what is best for you in the long run and there will always be sacrifices that needs to be made. You can still call and visit them to ensure their support towards your decisions. Convince them what is best for your future and I am sure that they will support you.

你的家人會理解你的，無論何時，他們都會支持你。當你有困難的時候，家庭就是你的庇護港，我相信你的家人不會阻止你職業生涯的進展。不過沖突往往也在家庭中發生，家人希望孩子能多和他們在一起，但有時因工作需要，必須去其他地方。當然，總有一天，他們會理解孩子，家人希望自己的孩子獨立的同時，也希望他們近在咫尺。您必須確定你想要的是什麼，從長遠來看，總需要犧牲某一方面。但你還可以隨時打電話給他們，探訪他們，以確保他們對你的決策給與支持。說服他們什麼是最適合你的未來，我相信他們一定會支持你的。

8. So you found a good job and a good wife, but you know you can't eat your cake and have it too. What would you choose?

    當你遇到一份好的職業和一位好的太太，魚與熊掌不能兼得，該選擇誰？

    If you have a good wife, she will always understand your situation and will give you the necessary support. She will try to help you to grow in your career and this is actually also for her own good as well as yours. If you have a good job, the two of you can have a better life in the future. There are sacrifices we have to make in life and there is no free lunch. If a good wife can see what is best for the family, I am sure she will support her husband to do well and succeed in his job.

如果你有一位好太太，她會理解你的處境也會支持你。她會幫助你在事業上進步，這對她來說也是有好處的。因為如果你有好的工作，你倆的將來生活也會更好。當然，生活中一定有人要做出一些犧牲，天下沒有免費的午餐。如果她能看到這樣對整個家庭有益，我相信她一定會支持你去做好你的工作。

9. How old should I be before I get married?
我應該多大才結婚啊？

Fate will determine when you get married. First of all, you will need to meet the right person who can be your friend. Someone who you can share your ups and downs with; who you can rely upon and trust when you are in trouble, who can take care of you when you are sick, who can help you to train your children well for the society, who will encourage you when it is needed, and who can give you a comfortable home where you feel safe. I do not think age makes any difference. My wife and I found each other when we were 40. So, best learn to spend time and understand more about your partner.

命運會決定你幾時結婚。首先，你要先遇到合適的對象，她/

他是你可以分享、依賴和信任的朋友，她/他會在你生病的時候照顧你，她/他有能力照顧教育好你們的孩子，會在你需要鼓勵的時候鼓勵安慰你，給你一個舒適的庇護所。我不認為結婚年齡是一個很大的問題，我和我太太也是在我們40歲才相遇，最好能用多一些時間先來了解你的伴侶，祝你好運。

10. Will marriage make me happier?
    婚姻會讓我更快樂嗎？

If you find someone as I have described above, then I am sure it will. Marriage is not a means for finding one's happiness but it is a commitment to another person, no matter how good or bad. Being happy with your partner does not require marriage but when you want to have children then it is best to provide them with a comfortable and safe home to grow up in, where both of you can fulfill your obligations as parents. That is when you must consider marriage.

如果你找到以上我講的那個人，我相信你一定會快樂。婚姻並不等於更快樂，婚姻是一種對他人的承諾，不論這是好還是壞。和你的伴侶快樂生活並不一定需要婚姻，但當你們有了孩子以後，這是保護孩子最好的方式，讓他們能在一個穩定，安全的家庭中成長。而你倆也可盡到為人父母的責任，也會讓你們的生命更加豐富，這就是你要認真考慮婚姻的時候。

11. How can I be a great person without sacrificing my life and family at the same time?

我要怎樣才可以成為一個偉大的人同時又不用犧牲自己的生活和家庭？

Even if you can be a great person, you still need to spend time with your family. You work hard at being a great person. You will need to be great at home too. Do not stop communicating with your family.

即使成為一個偉大的人，你仍需要花時間陪伴你的家人，不要停止與家人溝通。

12. If my friend wishes to get married next year but has not decided whether to have the wedding in Hong Kong or abroad; and he and his girlfriend cannot reach any conclusion, what should they do? He only saved $10,000 at the moment, is that enough?

如果我的朋友希望明年結婚，但現在他還不知道是去海外辦婚禮還是在香港。他和他的女朋友談過，還是不能下結論，他目前的積蓄不夠，因為他只有大約一萬元。他要怎樣才可以解決這個問題呢？

He can do a lot with $10,000. They can opt for a destination wedding that is equally just as memorable as a traditional wedding. I think the purpose of a wedding is also to create memorable moments for the newlyweds. So it is their decision on how to create this memorable moment, which they will share for the rest of their lives. Money cannot help one to do that. Different types of weddings can result in joy and happiness for different couples.

一萬元其實可以做很多事情了，他可以有一個很美好的旅行婚禮，這同樣是很有意義的。 我認為婚禮可以為新婚夫婦創造一個難忘的回憶，讓他們自己決定如何在他們的生活中創造這個難忘的時刻，他們可以永遠記住，而不是要用多少錢才可以幫你做到，不同的婚禮形式都可以是很美好的。

13. When considering and planning for children, besides the costs of each child being $4million, what else do we need to consider?

考慮是否要有小孩的時候，除了每個孩子需要四百萬元外，我們還應該關注什麼呢？

Essentially, I think you need to discuss with your partner about having children or not and starting your own family. It is a huge responsibility. It is not only a money issue. Raising and nurturing a child is more important than money. Are both of you ready for a child? It is fun to see the child growing up but it is a lot of work. Do you have the time and energy to enjoy and teach the child from right and wrong? Loving a child is one thing but teaching a child is another. It is you and your partner's full responsibility to ensure the proper growth of the child in a correct manner. Think thrice before you decide.

我想你首先要與你的伴侶認真地討論這個問題，養育孩子是一重大責任，不僅僅是金錢的問題。孩子的教育比金錢更為重要。 你們首先要確定是否雙方都準備好要孩子。孩子長大的過程是很開心的，但也有很多困難。你要有時間和精力去享受和陪伴孩子，教導孩子什麼是對是錯。愛孩子是一回事，但教孩子是另一回事，這完全由你和你的伴侶負責，以確保孩子的成長道路是正確的，在你決定之前一定要考慮清楚。

14. Would you rather live alone forever with great health, or live with a warm family yet have an incurable disease? Why?

您是願意永遠有健康但一個人生活呢，還是有一個溫暖的家庭卻同時有一個不治之癥？為什麼?

I will choose a warm family. No one lives forever. A warm family will give you love and care. When you have an incurable disease, you will need the care from your family. As long as you fulfill all your responsibilities in life i.e. to your family, children, friends, it is just as important you choose to live a happy life, and it does not need to last forever.

我會選擇一個溫暖的家庭，因為沒有人可以永遠活着，而溫暖的家庭可以帶給你愛和關心。當你患了不治之癥，你會非常需要家庭的關，只要你對家庭、孩子、朋友履行了你應盡的義務和責任。生活得開心更為重要，而不是要永遠活着。

15. Nowadays, many young people prefer to live in big cities, which is away from their hometown yet they also hope to take care of their parents as well. How does one balance the two?

現在很多年輕人喜歡待在大城市，遠離家鄉，但同時又希望能照顧到他們的父母，怎樣在兩者間取得平衡呢？

You may have more opportunities in big cities. However, you will face greater competition. I trust that most parents prefer their children to be independent and capable of taking care of themselves instead of taking care of their parents. They want their children to create a better life. If you can do that, you had already satisfied their needs and they will be happy. Surely, on occasions you can visit them or just give them a call. I am sure they welcome your call and want to know that you are OK. Parents will take care of themselves with their own friends. As long as you are doing well, they will be happy and they will be proud of you.

大城市通常會多些機會，同時也會有更強的競爭。我相信很多父母都會希望孩子能獨立而不是在家裏照顧他們，他們希望孩子們能有更好的生活。如果你能做到這一點，你已經滿足了他們的要求，他們會因此而高興。當然你應該要經常回去看看他們，或者打電話給他們。我相信他們會很希望接到你的電話，並且知道你一切都安好。父母只要有他們的朋友在一起，他們可以自己照顧自己，只要你生活工作順利，他們就會開心也會為你感到自豪。

16. What is the definition of success?
人生成功的定義是什麼呢？

Success is relative and determined by others. Others may think I have a successful life but I do not feel that I am successful. On the contrary, I feel that I am not successful and because of this, it will inspire me to work harder. Then, I can do more for others and achieve new heights. It is all relative; and it depends on whom you compare your success with. Others' idea of success may be very different from your idea of success. I always feel that I only achieved certain objectives in my life e.g. completion of a degree, a project, or writing a book. There are always other objectives down the road. I will try to achieve as many objectives as I can in my lifetime. It is up to others to determine whether my achievements are successful or not. I feel that I am happier than many of my super-rich friends. They may make more money than me and they are more successful in that sense, but I live a happier life because I can have freedom. I can enjoy the simplest things in life like having a bowl of noodles on the street, where my super-rich friends cannot. So in that sense, am I more successful in life? It is important to treasure each and every achievement in life, as it is something that no one can ever take away from you.

成功是相對的，是由他人來評定而非自己。其他人可能覺得我很成功，但我自己並不這樣認為。相反地，我覺得我並不成功，因此我才會更加努力工作，使我可以為他人做更多的事和再創新高。成功與否是相對的，取決於你和誰作比較。他人認為的成功或與你的成功定義有很大的分別。我總覺得我只能每一時段面向一定的目標，例如完成一個學位，一個項目，寫完一本書等等。接下來人生永遠會有新的目標，我會完成我人生中各個時段的不同目標。我的成就是否算得上成功，這是要由他人來評價的。我覺得我的人生可能比一些超級富豪的朋友更加開心，他們或許賺的錢比我多，但我擁有比他們更快樂的生活。我可以隨意地享受人生中最簡單的事情，例如我可在街上享用一碗麵而他們不能。我是否比他們在人生中更成功呢？珍惜你在人生中所得到的每一個成果更為重要，這是沒有任何人可以從你手中奪走的。

點
解

My Sharing
我的分享

Family remains the fundamental core of one's life. Everything you work for will be for the family. You will share your rewards with family. You will work hard to provide for your love ones and to create your own family. You will spend time and resources to nurture your offspring. You want your offspring to have a better life than you. However, miscommunication can cause misunderstanding between family members and even good intentions turn into anger and frustration. Conflicts may accumulate to a breaking point of no return. One will often need to choose wisely and learn to balance the value of life.

家庭是人生核心的重要部份，你所有的努力都是為了家庭，你希望與你心愛的家人分享你的成果。你努力打造自己的家，花費時間和資源來養育你的下一代，當然希望你的下一代會比你有一個更美好的人生。然而，溝通不暢經常導致家庭成員之間有不同的誤解，原本是良好的初衷卻變成憤怒和令對方沮喪，矛盾積累到不可協調，所以每個人總需要不時地調節和平衡人生的價值觀。

One shall not put themselves in a position where one needs to choose between family and work, or parents and future family. You need to decide and follow your own path and destiny. Marriage should not be imposed upon two people but is rather a willing union of two people. The realities of life will dictate when you shall set up your own family and when you have children. Work opportunities are plentiful so family must always be first. All parents are always there to help their offspring. You always have a sanctuary whenever you need it. So begin to share your problems with your parents. They will show more support and are more than happy to share your happiness and sorrows.

不要讓自己置於在家庭和工作之間，或現有家庭和未來家庭之間作出選擇，每個人是可以決定自己的命運。婚姻應該是雙方共同喜悅的結合，而不是要滿足父母的要求，現實會決定你何時建立自己的家庭和擁有自己的子女。工作機會永遠有很多，永不能超越家庭的重要性。所有的父母都會盡自己的能力協助子女，只要有需要的時候，你永遠都可以尋求父母的幫助，不用猶豫與你父母分享你的煩惱，他們會很樂意分享你的快樂和悲傷。

Country
國家

You must be part of or belong to a country in order to enjoy the comfort and warmth of a home. When one has a comfortable home, you shall have peace and prosperity. When a country is strong, its citizens and people will be respected and will not be looked down upon by others. It is the responsibility of all citizens to support their own country and be proud of their homeland.

有國才有家，要想有溫暖的家，首先要有一個穩定的國家。而當我們有了一個舒適的家，才有和平和繁榮。當國家強大時，人民才會得到尊重，不會被別人看不起。所有的公民都有責任支持自己的國家，為祖國感到自豪。

Different people with different views express their political views in different ways. All politicians want to convince others to support their own views. Every issue always has its own supporters and opposition. In politics, it is a matter of compromise before issues can be resolved.

不同的人對政治有不同的觀點和表達方式，政客們都想說服別人支持他們的觀點。但每一個問題總會有他的支持者和反對者，所以在解決問題之前，政治妥協是關鍵。

In recent years, the young people of Hong Kong have begun to participate in politics. Some are very much involved in various political activities. In reality, the participants all want to contribute to our society and country. Many have their own dreams and aspirations as to what should be the future for our society. They may even put their own thinking into action before considering all of the benefits and costs to others in a particular issue. Most disagreements or difference in opinions can reach the stage of compromise by communication and finding balance for all parties. The actions of young people or political activists often create the wrong results from what they intended, consequently not knowing they have made irreversible mistakes affecting their future and their lives. Subsequent acts of violence or even criminal acts can cause detrimental damage to their lives, which has totally deviated from the original intention of contributing to society and country. The only result it brings is they will not being appreciated nor supported by the community.

近年來，很多香港的年輕人開始關注政治，有些人非常積極參與各種政治活動。事實上，所有的參與者都想為我們的社會和國家做出貢獻。很多人對於社會的期望都有自己的想法，他們甚至未有綜合地考慮到各方利益和代價，就把自己的想法付諸行動。意見分歧需要通過溝通而達成共識，從而達到平衡，他們的行為往往造成錯誤的結果，犯一些不可逆轉的錯誤，而影響他們以後的人生。他們可能因做出一些暴力事件而被訴諸於法律，這些結果與他們的初衷背道而馳，並沒有貢獻社會和國家，最終的結果變成他們不被欣賞，也不被社會認同。

There are many questions raised by our young people. I hope my answers can inspire them so that they can follow the proper footsteps and continuously contribute to our society in the future. 我們的年輕人提出了很多問題，我希望在我的回答中可以啟發他們，讓他們能沿着正確的方向繼續為社會做出貢獻。

Questions & Answers:
問題與答案

1. Hong Kong is a tourist paradise. I do not understand why some local people object to Mainland tourists coming to spend in Hong Kong. It is obvious that with the completion of the high-speed rail, it will expand Hong Kong into the China market. Now, the Causeway Bay shop rent has dropped from one million dollars a month to five hundred thousand a month and still no one is interested. Retail is in recession. Jewelry shops are closing down. Pharmacies are moving. Even though the high spenders cause inflation, they also help the economy and create jobs. So how to balance this situation?

香港其實係一個旅遊勝地，唔明點解會有咁多所謂本土人士反對大陸客來港消費，就例如高鐵建成後，好明顯會打通內地市場，點解會搞到面臨爛尾，銅鑼灣地鋪由100萬月租到而家50萬都冇人租，零售業慘淡，金鋪關門，藥房搬遷，有錢旅客瘋狂購物係抬高咗物價，不過同時都帶旺經濟，創造就業，呢樣又係點衡量？

Some local people are afraid that if there are too many people coming from China, it will change their way of life in Hong Kong. In fact, their misconception is that these are only tourists who do not live in Hong Kong. Some people may have their own political agenda and localisation is one of their agendas on their campaign. They will try to manipulate the innocent thinking of young people and try to discredit visitors from China. It is all politics. The high-speed rail has its own problems. It exceeded its original budget and there were problems with the design and the planning in construction. The format of the contract was also not done properly. There were both supervision and design problems. This only gives more fuel for the opposition to blame the government. Fortunately, the revised budget was approved; if not, it would be detrimental to the Hong Kong people since they will have to face skyrocket claim. Hong Kong will need to face these immature political situations. It will cost Hong Kong dearly and may be that is what Hong Kong needs in order to realise that being in a state of political disagreement may not be good for Hong Kong. Hong Kong has been prosperous for the last 30 years. Many young people have no experience of the hard times in Hong Kong. They may need to experience this before they can come to their senses. That is why, in a society, there are always ups and downs and we all have to accept this as reality.

有些本土人士擔心的是如果有太多人來自國內，將會改變他們在香港的生活方式。而實際上他們誤解了，這些人只是來旅遊，並不是長住在香港的。有些人士他們有自己的政治議程，利用本土概念只是其中一個議程。他們只是利用了年輕人的單純，試圖抹黑中國的遊客，這都是一些基本政治抹黑。高速鐵路項目確實有其本身的問題，它超出了原預算和時間，設計和施工安排上都存在基本的問題，合同的安排也沒有做得很好，也有監督和設計上的問題，這些都給了反對派攻擊政府的藉口。幸運的是，修訂後的預算被立法會批准了，如果沒有批出，這將不利於全體香港人，因為他們將要面對多宗高額索賠。香港必須面對這些不成熟的政治形勢，這些會讓香港付出一定的代價，或許只有這樣，香港人最終才會明白到政治糾紛對香港沒有好處。香港在過去的30多年迅速發展，很多年輕人根本沒有經歷過香港困難的時期，他們可能需要經歷一下，才能明白實況。在每個社會都會有人往前行而有人拖後腿，我們也必須接受這個現實。

2. How do you evaluate Hong Kong and Mainland China students?
   你怎麼評價香港的學生和內地的學生？

Mainland students tend to be more prepared to learn and want to learn more. They have the eagerness to learn and improve themselves. Hong Kong students have been fortunate to experience prosperity for the last 30 years and have not had to face the downturn of the economy so life has been good in Hong Kong. I hope Hong Kong students will learn more regardless of the market conditions of our economy. The society is moving forward. Without learning, one will not progress in life and others will move ahead of you.

大陸的學生有學習的欲望，他們很渴望學習和提升自己。香港的學生擁有香港過去三十年積累的經濟財富，他們沒有經歷過香港經濟困難的時期，沒有經歷過低潮。我希望香港學生多學習，不要只看目前現有的經濟環境。整個社會是要往前進步的，一個人如果不懂得學習是不會進步，而其他人會趕上並超越與你。

3. Will you consider Mainland immigrants coming to Hong Kong as taking away the resources of Hong Kong?
    你會不會認為內地新移民是在搶掠香港的資源呢？

No, I believe many mainlanders will learn what Hong Kong has and will bring the goodness of Hong Kong back to Mainland China. Many also contribute and come to Hong Kong to construct a better future for Hong Kong. They will create a better China for our next generation. China needs to be strong in order for other countries to respect Chinese people. As a Chinese, we must want our country to be strong, otherwise others will look down on you. I've lived overseas for 15 years during which that time China was weak and poor. As Chinese people, others always bullied us. Nowadays, China is strong and is being recognised worldwide. I trust that no Chinese will be bullied anymore. We have an obligation to help our country and all mainlanders who study in Hong Kong will contribute to our country and to the Hong Kong society. So as a HongKonger, you also need to contribute to your country in order to make our country strong so others will not look down on Chinese people. It is up to you to perform so that Chinese people can be respected. During University, you will find that your lifelong friends are from your university years. Your

點
解

mainlander University friends will be your lifelong friends who may help you in the future when you need to work in China so treasure your friendships with them. People say when you are not at home you will need to rely upon your friends. Who will be better than your lifelong friends from university? They will help the Hong Kong students grow up faster when they are away from their sheltered life in Hong Kong. One needs to have a long term vision in life. We cannot only look at the present and ignore the benefits for the future. In addition, sharing is also one of the greatest joys in life. We mustn't forget that Hong Kong is only a small place with a population of 7 million whereas China has 1.4 billion people. The China market is huge and surely cannot be ignored in this generation or the next.

不會，我相信很多國內人會將香港好的東西帶回中國國內，其他國內人來港，共同建設一個美好的香港。他們將為我們的下一代創造一個更好的中國。中國富強，其他國家才會尊重你。作為中國人，我們必須祝願我們的國家富強，否則別人會看不起你。我在海外生活15年的時候，中國正處於軟弱和貧窮，作為中國人，我們經常會被人欺負。如今，中國富強是世界公認的，我相信，中國人現在不會再被別人不公平的欺負了。我們必須幫助我們的國家，所有在香港學習過的內地人也會報效於祖國和香港。我們在香港的人也要祝願我們的國家更富強，中國便不會再被別人看不起了，這取決於大家的表現，証明中國人是要受人尊敬的。至於在大學內，你會發現你一生中最好的朋友很大部分都是來自你的大學時代，你的國內同學朋友將會是你一生的朋友，當你需要在國內工作的時候，他們會幫助你，所以你應該珍惜他們的友誼。很多人都說出外靠朋友，誰會比你在大學時建立的友情更穩固呢？這將幫助香港學生在遠離香港的時候能夠快速成長。一個人需要有遠觀，我們不可以只看現在，而忽視未來的機會。此外，分享也是人生中最大的快樂。別忘了，香港只有700萬人口，而中國有14亿人。中國的市場是巨大的，特別是對於你們這一代和以後的人來說。

4. What is the future for Hong Kong?
   香港的前景如何？

I believe Hong Kong will continue to prosper. This is the only place in China that the Common Law is applicable and is a unique international city. It is the gateway to China and will continue to be so. It will always be an international city. There will always be ups and downs but Hong Kong people are very flexible and adaptable. They have strong resilience to problems and change quickly. I trust Hong Kong remains to be one of the best places to live in the world.
我相信香港會持續發展的，這是中國唯一使用普通法的城市，也是一個非常國際化的城市，這是進入中國的門戶。香港會有起與落，但香港人有很強的適應和變通能力，對於問題通常都能快速反應並解決，我相信香港仍然會是世界上其中一個最適宜居住生活的城市。

5. What are your views on the passing of Article 23 of the Basic Law?
   你對通過基本法第二十三條的看法如何？

This is something that will happen eventually and it's part of our duty as the people of Hong Kong to let it so. It is part of our mini-Constitution, the Basic Law. To protect one's country is the obligation of any country citizen. It is not a matter of choice. There is nothing wrong to have a law to protect your own country. They have similar laws in the USA, UK and other countries. We need to protect our country against all foreign aggression in order for our country to be strong and our people to live well. Other countries will not protect you. I lived in Canada for 15 years and I know that in order for Chinese to stand tall, our mother country needs to be modernised. Our people need to live well and we need to improve ourselves continuously. The same applies for an individual. China has moved forward tremendously in the last 20 years and the rest of the world are starting to notice. One cannot think of China as it was still back in the Cultural Revolution days. One must visit and learn about modern China. There are good and bad things in China. It is up to us to provide constructive ideas to make progressive change. China cannot change overnight and it will not happen like that. China has 1.4 billion people and it will take time. I trust that China is moving in the right direction at the moment, China is different. China already has its own identity and we shall have a system that suits China and no other. No single system is perfect. We can only use what we have. Stability is the key to any economic growth and that is important for Hong Kong and for China. We must maintain this as one of our core values.

這是一件勢在必行的事，而且也是公民責任的一部份。
二十三條也是基本法屬於我們香港小憲法的一部分。保衛自
己的國家是每個國家公民應盡的義務，這不是一個可供選擇
的問題，有一條法律來保護自己的國家絕對是沒有錯。無論
在美國、英國或者其它國家都有相似的法律，我們必須保護
我們的國家不受外來的攻擊。保障國家強大，人民才可以
安居樂業。其它國家是不會保護你的。我在加拿大生活了15
年，中國人要抬得起頭來。我們的國家必須實行現代化，人
民需要生活好，同時我們也要不斷地提升自己。中國在過去
的20年已經有了翻天覆地的改變。這一點是全世界都應該看
到的。人們不應該還把中國想像成為以前文革那時的樣子。
多了解和游覽中國，中國有好的也有壞的地方。我們可以提
供更多有建設性的方法幫助它變得越來越好。它不可能一天
就完全改變過來，這是不可能的。中國有14億人口，需要時
間來改變。但至少它目前是往正確的道路上發展。中國是與
別國不同的，它有自己的特性，我們應該有一套獨特和與之
互相適應的制度。沒有任何一個制度是完美的，我們只能使
用我們現有的。穩定是所有經濟發展的關鍵因素。這一點對
中國和香港都非常重要，這也是我們的核心價值之一。

6. Do you think Hong Kong is still politically stable?
    你認為香港的政治穩定嗎？

Yes, Hong Kong is still politically stable. China will not
allow Hong Kong to be unstable. Hong Kong is much better
than many places in the world. Freedom House (USA)
and Fraser Institute (Canada's top think tank) rank Hong
Kong as one of the freest economies in the world. We have

點解

freedom of currency, freedom of speech, freedom of travel and we are one of safest place in the world. After you travel around the world, you will find Hong Kong is the best place of all. I personally travelled to many places and Hong Kong is still my home and I treasure Hong Kong very much. We need to be constructive and contribute to Hong Kong. I am sure you do not trash and litter in your own home. Hong Kong is our home and we need to keep it that way.

是的，香港政治上是穩定的，國家不會讓香港不穩定，香港已經比世界很多地方要好很多。香港被美國自由之家和弗雷澤研究所（加拿大的頂級智庫）評選為世界上最自由的地方之一。我們擁有貨幣自由、言論自由、出入自由，是世界最安全的地方之一。當你在世界各地遊覽過之後，你會發現香港是最好的地方之一。我個人遊覽過很多地方，但香港仍是我的家而且我會珍惜它。我們要有建設性地去幫助和建設香港，為香港做貢獻。我相信你不會想在自己的家裏亂扔垃圾，而香港是我們的家，要保持這樣下去。

7. Have you ever had a moment of political differences and perspectives from your friends, colleagues or family members, and how would you deal with it?

你有沒有曾經與你的朋友，同事或者家庭成員有不同的政見，你會怎樣處理呢？

Surely, one needs to accept other's views, but you do not need to agree with them. Everyone is entitled to have his or her own opinion. Some are more right than others. Focus on your studies and improve yourself in your career before getting involved into politics. Politics is for someone to contribute, and it is difficult to make a living out of it. Have an open mind. Be your own judge. Do what is best for your studies and career. If you come across a person with different perspectives and if you still want to be friends with that person, it is best to avoid discussion on political views. I have good friends with different perspectives. As long as you are good to them, they will respect you as friends.

經常會有，你應該接受別人的意見，但並不需要每一個都同意。每個人都有他表達意見的權利，他人的意見可是對或錯。在你想參與政治以前，先要專注於你的學業和自己的前途，政治是貢獻社會而非一門職業。保留一個開放的思維和自我判斷的能力，為你自己的學業和前途作出最大的努力。如果你遇到一個有不同政治觀念的人，如果你仍然想和他做朋友，最好的方法是不要和他過多的談論政治立場。我有很多好朋友與我有不同觀點，但只要你對他們好，他們也會尊重你為他們的朋友。

8. Somehow, the Hong Kong Government and the Chinese Government have way too many public issues making Hong Kong socially unstable. What are your views?

不知為何，香港政府和中國政府常有很多公眾問題，使香港社會不穩定，你意見如何？

Hong Kong is still one of the safest places in the world. We are also one of the freest economies and place to live in the world, ranked by the Fraser Institute in Canada and Freedom House (USA). We have freedom of speech, freedom of money flow, freedom of travel, law & order, a sound legal system, free trade and a gateway to the largest economy in the world. You have to understand how China operates to understand its government. You need to learn about China. This is essential for your generation. It is not a matter of choice, it is a necessity. If you look at it from the viewpoint of a parent (China) rather than from the point of view of us (HK), you will understand their views. There is always reason for anyone's action. We live under the roof of this family (Chinese Government) so it's not a matter of choice.

香港仍然是世界上最安全的地方之一，我們是世界上最自由的地方之一，這是由加拿大的弗雷澤研究所和美國自由之家公佈出來的。我們有言論的自由，有資金流動的自由，可以自由旅行，有良好的秩序，良好的法律體系，自由貿易的權力，位於世界通往最大經濟體的門戶。你要了解中國是如何運轉的，才可了解他們。你需要認識中國，這對你們這一代是非常重要的，這不是一個可以選擇的問題，而是必須的。如果你以父母的觀點來看待中國，而不是用我們自己的觀點來看問題，你會更能明白為什麼中國要這樣做。他們的反應全是有原因的，我們是中國的一部份，而這並不是一個選擇。

9. Many young people talk about our ex- Chief Executive. They said that he is a liar and say that they will never go to China. On the other hand, I think of people like Wong Chi Fung. Will Hong Kong be put into chaos by these people? I do not understand how they think.

很多年輕人都在討論我們的前特首，都話特首係大話精，都話一世都唔會返國內。但我又諗到黃之峰等人，香港未來會唔會俾呢幫人搞死？真係唔明白佢地係點諗的。

I think the Chief Executive has many concerns and he has the heart to build a better tomorrow for Hong Kong. If a young person is not prepared to go to China in his life, he only limits himself in his own potential to grow. He needs to realise the opportunities and possibilities of expansion into the huge market of China. Everyone determines their own destiny. No one can force another to do things that they do not want to do. Wong Chi Fung has his own political agenda. He does what he does for his own reasons. He cannot excel in his studies and he needs other things to achieve his political ambition. He motivated others to support his objective and tried to achieve his own goal. Hong Kong people should be mindful of this and should know how to determine Hong Kong's destiny.

我覺得行政長官有很多事情要關注，他是一名有心來建設一個美好香港的特首。如果年輕人沒有準備好去中國，他們只會把自己困在香港，受限於香港的發展。不去中國接受更多和更大的發展空間，沒有機會開發更大的市場，這對他們自己來講是很大的損失。每個人要決定他自己的命運，沒有人能逼你做自己不想做的事情。黃之峰有他自己的政治目標，他做的這一切都是為他自己的決策，他在學業上並不出色，他需要在其它事情上來完成他的政治野心。他激奮其他人支持他，以便有一天能達到他自己的目標。作為成年人，我們應該能看清楚和明白這些。香港人是有警覺性的，我們會知道如何決定香港的前途和未來的。

10. In recent year, many young people participate in civic movements to express their dissatisfaction on unfair treatment and sense of righteousness. Do you think they are causing disorder to Hong Kong?

近年開始，愈來愈多青年人參加社會運動，透過運動表達他們認為不公義和不公平的事，你會否覺得他們是在搞亂香港？

It is fine to express points of view in any civic action, but it needs to be done in a proper and lawful manner. No one will listen to someone who threatens others. That is not expression of views or freedom of speech. That is trying to force your views onto others. Do you like to be forced to accept other's view? I do not think so. If one wants to improve our society, one needs to express one's views through proper channels, giving views with reasons, views that are realistically workable. You may have a great idea but it takes time to change the system. The system in a country or in the Administration of Hong Kong existed before you and I were born. It will not be changed overnight. This is what I call the reality test in life. Anything is possible but it has to be realistic and practical. We, as engineers, always look to practical and workable solutions. It also needs to be accepted by the majority. One view is not enough. The view needs to balance the needs of all. If the view only satisfies a few, it will not be acceptable to the majority. There are also the concerns of the silent majority that one needs to address. Democracy is tailored for the majority and there are always opposing views in any social system. One needs to learn how to accept and balance the other's view. The system at present was formed based upon many years of workable solutions, and surely it can be improved but it takes time and can only be done progressively. Violence will never change the system. No government or the general public will accept violence. Violence can only damage one's future. If one sits back, you will realise that life is not always fair but it is up to you, to come out as a winner through the present system. It may not be totally fair to one but may be fair to another. If one only wants to fight the system, the system will not accept you and you will not be a winner. There are rules in any society just like the same in school. You need to pass your exams before you get your degree so that hopefully you will have a better start than others. All societies have basic rules that everyone abides by, otherwise would be chaos that will only damage the prosperity that was built up throughout generations. If there is chaos, there will not be economic growth. The only people who suffer are the ordinary people. It will not affect the rich or the people in power. We want prosperity for our people so that we can have a good living and be happy. We need to be content with what we have and shall not destroy what we already have. We need to be constructive and build a better tomorrow, and surely not by destroying what we already have to achieve this. If we do not treasure our present, how can one achieve a better tomorrow? Young people may not think of all the consequences when they try to present their ideas. Everything in life has a cost and consequences. Some can be damaging to the rest of one's life. I hope more guidance can be provided to our present youths and the young people of Hong Kong so they can avoid making the same mistakes in their lives.

每個人都可以在公民行動中表達自己的觀點，但它必需以適當和合法的方式來表達。沒有人會喜歡受別人威脅，這不是表達意見的方式，這是試圖將你的意見強加與別人，你願意在威脅下接受別人的觀點嗎？我不這樣認為。如果一個人想改善我們的社會，他一定需要通過正確的渠道來表達意見，要有理由的意見，切實可行的意見。你可能有一個偉大的提議，但需要時間來改變。現有的架構和系統在你我出生之前就已經在這個國家或在香港政府運行的了，它不會在一夜之間改變，這就是我所說的現實測試。任何事情都是可能的，但它必須是要現實和實際的。我們，作為一名工程師，我們要尋找出切實可行的解決方案，也同時是可以被人接受的方案，僅僅一個概念是不足夠的，觀點需要平衡所有人的需要。如果意見只滿足少數人，是不會被大多數人所接受的，同時應該顧及沉默的大多數人的需要。民主制度也只能為大多數人而設，在任何社會制度中都有反對的聲音，一個人需要學會如何接受別人的觀點或看法。目前的制度是建基於許多年的可行方案而形成的。當然制度永遠可以改良，與時並進，但需要循序漸進和時間。暴力永遠不會改變制度，任何政府或公眾市民都不會接受暴力，暴力只會損害一個人自己的未來。如果回顧一下，你會意識到，生活是不一定公平的，它可能對你來講不公平，但對於另一個人又是公平的。你要從現有的制度中勝出，才是一個真正的成功者。如果一個人只想打破現有制度，不會獲得認同，你不會成為贏

家。在每一個社會裏都有着如在學校裏一樣的規則。你想要
得到某個學位,首先你要通過考試,這樣你才可能會有一個
更好的起步點。所有的社會都有規律,每個人都必須遵守否
則會有混亂,混亂只會破壞社會繁榮。如果有混亂,就不會
有經濟增長和發展,唯一受苦的人是老百姓,而不會影響到
富人或當權者。我們希望社會繁榮,能夠使每個市民有良好
的生活環境和幸福感,就應該珍惜現有的而不是要破壞。我
們需要的是有建設性地建設一個更美好的明天,當然不是通
過破壞來建立一個更好的明天。如果我們不珍惜我們現有
的,又何來能實現更好的明天呢。年輕人在提出一些想法
時,可能沒有考慮清楚後果和代價,生命中的每一件事都有
一定的成本和代價,有些可能會嚴重影響他們自己的一生。
我希望能為我們香港的年輕人做出多一些好的指引,使他們
不會犯出追悔莫及的錯誤。

11. When we encounter a terrorist attack, what responsibilities should one's government bear?
當我們遇到恐怖襲擊時,政府應承擔什麼責任?

Terrorist attacks are the result of different viewpoints of extremists. One shall never use violence to resolve differences. The public will never accept violence regardless of the cause. Whoever initiates violence will always lose in the end.
恐怖襲擊是極端不同觀點的結果,絕不應該使用暴力來解決
分歧。不論什麼原因,公眾永遠不會接受暴力,無論誰一旦
發起暴力,他最終一定會失敗。

12. Why do some countries have the death penalty to punish people and to stop them from killing others? One shall not harm another person. One shall only try to help others. That is what a good person should be. Does one have the right to terminate another's life?

為什麼在有些國家會用死刑懲罰殺人犯來證明殺人是錯誤的？每個人都不應該傷害他人，而應盡量幫助他人，這是一個好人的標準，一個人有權終結他人的生命嗎？

We are not God. The law is made by most of the people in one's country. It does not need to be agreed by all. The rest of the people need to follow the majority. That is how countries are being operated regardless of what systems are used. Many countries enforce the death penalty to deter and punish criminals from killing and taking the lives of others.

我們不是神，法律是代表了一個國家的主流觀點，這並不需要所有人的同意，其餘不同意的人也必須順應主流的決定。不論是在什麼體制的國家，這是一個國家運轉的根本元素之一。有很多國家都認為可用死刑，這可使殺人者知道殺人的後果來阻嚇他犯罪。

13. In recent year, the Hong Kong Government tried to promote national education and with recent scandals in China, most of the young people in Hong Kong do not seem to know their own national identity. Do you think this lack of understanding of national identity will have a negative effect to the future development of Hong Kong?

275

近年來，香港政府強推國民教育和中國政府接連爆出醜聞，香港青少年似乎對於國民身份的認同不增反跌，你是否覺得年輕人對國家歸屬感的下降會對香港的社會發展造成負面的影響？

I believe young people need to know the history of our country in order to perform better in the future years to come. If you know more, you will understand more and know where to find and take note of the opportunities it can provide. History tends to repeat itself, therefore, it is a good learning ground for any individual. The earlier you learn the history of your country, the earlier you will know your priority in life. You can achieve much more, much earlier. It is regrettable that our school system does not provide this as a compulsory course at the moment. In my early days, Hong Kong was a colony of Britain and we only studied the history of China up to the Qing Dynasty so I only learnt about Chinese history while I was working. I wish I had the opportunity to learn it in school. I could only learn it on my own while I was working. It has helped me to know where the opportunities are in our country and in Hong Kong. I am sure if the young people of Hong Kong do not know the history, the growth and the composition of our country, they are unable to take the opportunities that it offers. They will be left behind in life to face with competition from China and from overseas e.g. Singapore. I can assure you that one day they will regret it. If one does not understand the direction of China, it will be detrimental to one's career. The willingness

點
解

to learn is an important element in life. Willingness to learn will make one grow. What's most regretful is that many young people in Hong Kong lack this motivation and willingness to learn.

我相信年輕人應該要認知我們自己的歷史，要瞭解我們的國家。你知道得越多，越會理解，也會更容易找到機遇。為避免不好的歷史重演，我們每一個人都應該要瞭解歷史。越早知道歷史，認識自己的國家，你越能找到自己人生的優先次序。可悲的是，我們的學校目前還沒有將歷史作為必修課。在我那個年代，香港是英國的殖民地，我們只能學到清史。我是直到工作以後，才自修到我們中國建國的歷史。我多希望我在學校的時候已有機會學習到啊！而事實上我直到工作的時候才自學到，它幫助我知道中國和香港的機遇。我相信，如果香港的年輕人不學習歷史，國家的成長歷史，國家的組成，他們會被來自中國和其它海外國家如新加坡等國家的競爭者甩在身後。這樣總有一天他們是會後悔的。如果不瞭解中國的發展方向，將嚴重不利於他們的職業生涯。學習的意願是生活中的一個重要因素，願意學習會讓你成長。我注意到許多香港年輕人缺乏動力，這是最讓人遺憾的。

14. According to the policy in Singapore, every couple that just graduated can apply for an affordable apartment unit to live in while working. Can the HK government do something alike? Because sometimes it doesn't make any sense for me to work and struggle to buy property. The property prices are terrifying to me and I totally feel my effort is useless if I want to live in Hong Kong. I work overtime and my salary can never help me to get a place to live without help from my parents.

根據新加坡的政策，每對年輕夫婦一畢業即可申請住房，而且他們的收入也可以負擔得起，香港政府能不能也有類似的政策？因為很多時候，我雖然努力工作，而事實上是在為"地皮"工作，這很沒意義。房價是我無可能支付的，我覺得我的努力完全沒有希望，即使我再怎麼努力工作，沒有父母的幫助，我的收入根本不足以支撐我能負擔的一個棲身之所。

The HK government is aware of this problem and is doing everything it can to help young people with housing needs. One should not expect to have a house right after graduation. I did not buy my first home right after graduation. It took me more than a decade before I could pay up on the initial deposit. Singapore is different since their cost of land is much lower and a lot of land is reclaimed, which is not possible for Hong Kong. One can start with living a bit further away from town, like some live in Yuen Long, Tuen Mun etc., or even in Shenzhen. In New York, people live in New Jersey and commute to work in downtown New York. We need to accept this as a reality. Hong Kong is a very expensive place to live just like 5th Avenue in New York. We need to accept travelling time. In most countries, one needs to travel for at least an hour or more to work e.g. UK, Japan, Australia, and even in Beijing. We need to accept changes and make the best of it. I used to commute for an hour and half (one way) to work every day to my job site after graduating from engineering. Savings will get you your first home. Save up for the future.

點
解

香港政府已經意識到這個問題，並且一直在努力幫助年輕人解決他們的住房需求，所以他們很努力找適當的地。我認為年輕人不應該期望一畢業就可以買到房子，我也不是一畢業就買到房子。新加坡的情況不同於香港，因為他們的土地成本比香港低，而且他們開拓了很多土地如填海等，而這在香港是很困難的。我覺得年輕人可以住到離市區遠一些的地方，比如元朗、屯門等地甚至深圳。在紐約，很多在紐約工作的人住在新澤西。我們需要接受現實，香港的生活成本很高，就像紐約的第五大道，我們需要接受一定的交通時間。在很多國家，居民工作也都要花上超過一個小時的交通時間或者更多，比如在英國、日本甚至北京等地。我們要接受改變並接受現實，我過去剛畢業時也曾每天要花上1.5小時在路上才到工地上班。儲蓄可使你得到你第一個房子的夢想，從今天開始要為未來而儲蓄。

15. If I want to improve the world, should I work in business or politics?

如果我想對這世界作出改善做貢獻，我應該投身於商業還是政治方面？

You can improve the world in both. Businesses can help improve the world. You can help others when you can afford to do so. Politics is something you can get involved with after you have success in business or when you are able to fulfill most of your obligations in life. You may use the power of politics to influence others but it may not always lead you to achieve what you want. Politics is an art of negotiation. One can always contribute to the world through different ways or means.

我相信做生意和政治兩方面都可以幫助改善世界。做生意當
然能改善這個世界，你可以在有能力時幫助別人。政治是一
門需要你在自己的能力足夠強大後，以及滿足了人生中的責
任後才能涉足的。你可以通過政治的力量影響他人，但並不
是每個想做的事都能達到目的，政治是一門談判的藝術。每
個人都可以通過不同的方式為這世界做出貢獻。

16. Is there any situation that puts you in a dilemma due to political and work issues?
你有沒有因為政治問題和工作有兩難的時候？

Political issues are matters of your own choosing. It is most dangerous to get into such issues when you are not financially sound and it will not be worthwhile to go against the government. The government has many resources to contest with anyone. The structure of the government is there for a reason. Your losses will be much more than you can expect. Damages will not only be to yourself but to your family and your future generation. You can always make a choice in work. One is always in a dilemma with work issues. You have to comply with what your boss wants; otherwise you will not be successful. You have to go with the trend and follow what the company wants you to do. You can change jobs if you do not like it. This is the only recourse for you. If you stay with the company, you will need to fulfill what your boss needs and likes. You can have that opportunity if you are the boss.
政治問題是你自己的選擇，當你沒有雄厚的財力時，它會變

得非常危險，也沒有力量與政府對抗。政府永遠有比你更多的資源來與你鬥爭，這是政府的職能結構所在。你的損失將遠比你可預見的要大，而這些損失也不僅在於你自己，更可能涉及你的家人和下一代。在工作問題上，你永遠有選擇權。任何人在工作中都會有兩難的情況，你必須要按照你老板的要求否則你就不會成功，你必須跟隨趨勢以及公司的期望。如果你不喜歡，那你可以換一份工作，如果你要待在這家公司，你就必須要滿足你老板的期望。如果你是老板，那情況就不同了。

17. How can we trust our leaders if they don't believe in us?

如果我們的領導人對我們沒信心，我們又如何可以信任他呢？

To start with, your leader reached his or her position for a reason, either by way of election or appointment for a reason. All leaders have their own mandates in life. They go into politics for a purpose. Some may want the position to achieve new heights, some may want to progress in their career, some treat it as the best job in the world; some may want to contribute and do something more for the community. Everyone has different views or opinions on issues. Your leader also has his or hers. One needs to respect other's opinion and compromise. That is politics. There are trade offs in every policy. You may express your views but not everyone will agree with you. You can always try to convince others through proper means. You have to accept that you may not have considered all the specific issues of the bigger picture. Your leader may have other information that you may not have to make a decision. Different views are important but the bigger picture and to accept the decision of the majority may often times prove to be an even greater challenge than accepting one's views. Accepting other's views may sometimes be a better option unless you can prove that your views are more convincing than others.

不論如何，你的領導人能坐到他這個位子上必有他個人的獨特之處，不論他是直選或委任。領導人都有他自己的願望和訴求，他也是為了某些個人目標才進入政壇。有些人可能希望通過這個位子可以取得更高的職位，有些希望職業生涯更上一層樓，有些認為這是一份收入不錯的工作，有些人可能想為社會做些事，想貢獻自己的經驗和力量。每個人都可能對某些政策有不同的觀念，你的領導人也同樣如此，雙方都應該尊重他人的意見。你可以表達自己的觀點但不是每個人都會同意你的觀點。你可以通過正當合法渠道去盡力說服別人，政治是不同的妥協。你也要接受自己可能在某些角度沒能看到大局的觀點，你的領導人可能獲知其它你所不知道的資訊，來作出決定。不同的觀點當然重要，但大局更為重要，盡量接受他人的觀點，除非你有能力證明和說服他人你的觀點比他的強。

點
解

My Sharing
我的分享

The future of the young person depends on the effort of the individual. Self reliance is essential in order to achieve one's dream. One firstly needs to complete his work on hand through hard work. A good social network will help one to explore future opportunities. Opportunities always exist just around the corner.

年輕人的未來，取決於個人的努力。為了實現自己的夢想，自力更生是至關重要。首先，需要通過辛勤工作完成自己的工作，同時建立良好的社交網絡，有助於探索未來的機會，而機會永遠就在轉角處。

Many young people worry that their quality of life will diminish when there are too many visitors coming to Hong Kong. They worry that they can no longer decide on their future. They worry that the cost of living will increase. On the other hand, more visitors coming to Hong Kong will help the economy and increase employment. Politicians always use these individual issues to contest with the Administration of the government. Politicians use slogans, judicial reviews and filibuster tactics to cause substantial delays in the approval process of future projects, resulting in subsequent damages to the long-term interests of others. Politicians stir up short-term concerns to achieve their own political agenda.

很多年輕人擔心，太多遊客到來會讓他們的生活質素降低，他們擔心不再可以決定自己的未來，擔心生活費用增加。其實從另一方面來看，更多的遊客來港會幫助經濟發展，增加就業。可是很多政客總是用這些單一問題來攻擊政府，而沒有改善問題。利用政治口號，司法覆核，或拉布對未來的項目造成嚴重的延誤，損害市民的長遠利益。很多政客利用其短期的影響力來實現他自己個人的政治目的。

For the last 20-30 years, China has been progressing steadily. The people live better. Education levels in people have improved. Ample food supplies and basic needs are being fulfilled. The wheel of modernisation cannot turn back under any circumstances. International reputation has improved. China needs to be strong in order for other people to respect Chinese people. Chinese people can then hold their heads high and can face the many challenges of tomorrow. Every citizen of China will need to face these challenges. Political disputes occur continuously and will not stop with time. The fundamental resulting goal is that the people will get the benefits of the changes, improve upon their livelihood, and have political stability. In reality, the ordinary person does not really concern himself or herself with who governs them. The wishes and hopes of the people are that they have enough food on the table, maintain a happy and good living, and enjoy peace and safety. Anyone or party who can provide such needs to the people will sustain his or her leadership.

中國在過去的20至30年間，各方面都有穩步提升，人民生活更美好，教育水平提高，糧食供應充足，人民基本需求得到滿足。中國的現代化在任何的情況下都不會被扭轉了，國際聲譽大幅提升。中國強大了，別的國家才會尊重中國人，中國人可以抬起頭來，面對未來的挑戰，而每一個中國人都是要面對這些挑戰的。政治爭議總會不斷發生，不會因時間而停止，但最終的目標是要讓人民在變化中生活得更好，改善民生，實現政治穩定。其實大部份人並不關心誰是統治者，人民的意願是希望他們的餐桌上有足夠的糧食，有幸福美滿太平的生活。任何人或黨派如果可以為人民提供到這些需求的，便可以容易地維繫其政權的穩定。

As a Chinese citizen, we need to treasure what we have. Nothing comes easy. We shall progress and create our future. We all hope that our life will get better and not go backwards. Wrong or incorrect political agendas or directions can easily put the economy and the country in an adverse position or go in reverse. On the discussion of political issues, one needs to be reasonable and conduct themselves within lawful means and through proper channels. Any changes made need to cater for the majority and cannot be forced upon others. When one gets involved into political issues, one needs to firstly consider one's own capability in such issues. You need to do reality check before participating. You determine when is the best time to get involved and how to achieve the best results. Politics is only one of the many means to achieve one's objective. There are always other channels that one can contribute to achieve a similar objective on any issue.

作為中國公民，我們應該珍惜我們所擁有的，這是經過多年努力得來的。我們要逐步發展和創造我們的未來，我們都希望生活會更好，而不是在倒退。政治議題或方向走錯了，很容易

Friend

會使當地經濟和國家發展滑坡。在討論政治問題時，一定要在合情合理合法的情況下討論，也要通過適當的合法途徑。任何社會改變都需要照顧到大多數人的需要，而不能強加於人。當涉及到政治問題時，首先要考慮到自己在這個問題上的能量。在參與之前，你要做現實測試，考慮可行性，要找到參與的最佳時機，才能達到最好的成果。政治只是實現自己目標的其中一種手段，總是有其他方法來完成相同的目標。

Epilogue
總結

As I said in the Preface, it is wonderful to be young. We all have dreams, ambitions and aspirations. We want to achieve, accomplish, and accumulate. However, problems, troubles and obstacles that we need to overcome always challenge us. One may be affected by peer pressure and become impatient and look for short-term solutions. We need to be realistic and practical, and set goals that are achievable. To be able to master the techniques and skills of problem solving will become critical in one's life.

正如我在前言中所說，年青是美妙的。我們都有夢想，目標和抱負，我們想要逐一實現，完成和增值。然而，我們總是面臨着很多需要克服的問題、困難和障礙。一個人可能受到同輩壓力的影響，變得不耐煩，尋找短期解決方案。我們需要面對現實，並建立可以實現的目標，能夠掌握解決問題的手段和技巧對一個人的人生至關重要。

I had many dreams in my younger days. I wanted to be the best in my profession. I wanted to travel the world. I wanted to retire early. I wished I was the happiest person on earth. I wished I could be rich enough to afford whatever I needed in life. I wished I was a casanova. I wanted to build a unique building in my lifetime. I wanted to have my own company. I wanted to achieve my professional qualification as early as possible. I wanted a nice car. I wanted to go to the best restaurant in town and the list goes on.

我年輕時有過很多夢想，我想在事業上做到最好，早些退休，環遊世界，我希望我是世界上最開心的人，能擁有足以負擔我人生中一切所需的財富。我還希望我是一個美男子，人人喜歡。我夢想能在我一生中建造一座獨一無二的建築物，能發展自己的公司，能早日拿到我的專業資格，擁有一輛好車，能到香港最好的餐廳等等⋯⋯

In reality, I have only been able to achieve some of these and I did make some of my dreams come true. I have gone through hell and back to realise that some dreams are unrealistic and unnecessary. One always has to work for what one wants to have. Only hard work will bring you closer to your dreams. There is no free lunch for anyone. When others were working 8 hours a day, I was working 2 or even 4 hours more. The world owes you nothing. You create your own future.

而在現實中，我只能夠實現到其中一些夢想。我經歷過地獄般的日子，認識到有一些夢想是不切實際的，也是沒有必要的。每個人都需要努力工作才能得到願望中想要的東西，只有努力才能使你更接近你的夢想，天下沒有免費的午餐。當其他人每天工作八小時，我就比他們工作多二至四個小時。這個世界沒有人欠你，只有你自己才能創造出屬於你的未來。

You have to learn to continuously improve yourself in order to excel. It will enhance your memory and appreciation for life, and help you formulate thinking in different perspectives and directions. It will empower you with new, positive energies and the confidence and determination to become a better person. You need to constantly equip yourself so that you will be able to

點
解

grab the next available challenge in life. I used to and still attend various courses and seminars that are related to my work or interests.

你必須不斷學習，提升自己，讓自己更進步。學習可以幫你增強記憶力，享受生活，並使你可以用不同的視野和方向來思考問題。它還可以賦予你有新的正面能量，增強決心和信心，使你成為一個更優秀的人。你需要不斷地裝備自己，這樣你才可以迎接人生中的下一個挑戰。我過去到現在經常參加各類型與工作或興趣有關的課程和研討會，吸收新的知識和思維。

It is practically impossible to make everyone happy in your life. You only need to satisfy yourself and those you care about. Your own desires will drive you towards reaching your goals and dreams. For example, I needed to make enough money to buy my first Porsche car. No one really cares if you make it or not in life, except yourself. You need to have self-initiative in order to have achievements in life. Actions always speak louder than words. Start now and do not wait for the 'perfect' time. I have a friend who wanted to publish a book but he has never been able to do it. I never dreamt that I would be a writer yet this is my seventh published book.

在你的人生中不可能讓每個人都快樂，只能選擇滿足到你自己和你所關心的人，你的慾望會驅使你實現自己的目標和夢想。比如我以前需要賺足夠的錢來買我的一輛保時捷車。在你人生中，除了你自己，其它人不會理會你成功與否，你需要自發地做事。事實勝於雄辯，想做就做，不要等待完美的時機。我有一個朋友多年來想出版一本書，但他一直沒有做到。而我自己做夢也沒想到

我有一天會成為一名作者，但這本書已經是我出版的第七本書
了。

You must remember that no one will save you when you are in
trouble. You may want your family members to assist you, but
it surely is a bonus when they do, and not an obligation on their
part when they don't. You are on your own and you must rely on
yourself. You must equip yourself to face challenges in life. When
there are opportunities, after due consideration, you must take it.
Otherwise you will never succeed. You must pursue your desires
and goals with hard work, patience, and persistence. Do not
give up until you have achieved your goal. The greater the risk,
the bigger the reward. You need to be able to step out of your
comfort zone to achieve newer heights.

你必須記住當你有困難時沒有任何人必須要來拯救你，你或許希
望家人可以幫助你，但這並不是他們的義務。你只有依靠自己，
必須裝備好自己來面對人生中的挑戰。當有新的機會出現的時
候，經過適當的深思熟慮後，你必須抓住它，否則你永遠不會成
功。你必須努力工作，並且要有耐心和毅力來追求你的願望，不
能放棄，直到你達成自己的目標。要有高的回報就意味着有更大
的風險，你需要走出自己的舒適圈，才能走向新的高峰。

One needs to accept reality. We need to be prepared to accept
failure as part of our lives. You must not be defeated and learn
from failure and setbacks. You need to learn from your mistakes
and become better and stronger. You have to know when to stop.
You can be at the top of an organization but one day you will
need to step down. It is important that you know when you should

retire from a position and how succession be carried out for the betterment of the organisation. Everyone is replaceable including you. You should conserve your energy and be prepared for the next challenge in life. When you are confident, add courage and hard work, and success will be waiting for you just around the corner.

人要學會接受現實，要接受失敗是人生中不可避免的部份。勝之坦然，敗之淡然，你總有機會可以捲土重來。你不能被失敗擊潰，而要從失敗和挫折中學習。你要從錯誤中學習到失敗的原因和以後預防的方法，這些會讓你變得更好更強。你也要知道何時應該停下來，作為任何一個單位/公司/組織的負責人，總有一天是需要退下來的，所以關鍵是你要知道你何時應該從崗位上退下來，如何找到繼承者使單位/公司/組織得以持續發展。沒有人是無可取代的，包括你在內。你應該儲備你自己的能量，來準備迎接下一個新的挑戰。信心在，勇氣在，努力在，成功在！

Value your friends and co-workers, as they are your friends for life. They are the ones who will share experiences with you on your life journey. These friends can help you appreciate more in your life and share the joy of your successes. You should be kind to yourself and the people around you. There are many who are not as fortunate as you are. You should be thankful for what you have and what you have achieved. Everything has a price and you have to pay for it somehow, someday. You have to know your limitations in what you can and cannot do. You must not over stress since it only brings disappointment. Your personality and attitude can determine your future.

要懂得珍惜你的朋友和同事，他們是你一生的朋友，他們是在你的人生旅途中與你分享經驗的人，這些朋友可以幫助你欣賞人生，分享你成功的喜悅。你應該善待自己和周圍的人，有許多人不如你幸福，你應該感謝你所擁有的和你已取得的成就。凡事都有代價，你必須付出才有收獲。你必須知道哪些能做哪些不能做，盡自己所能及之事，你不應該過度逼迫自己，因為這樣只會讓你失望，靠自己的人品和性情來打造你的未來。

You must maintain your interests in life. This enables you to refresh and relax your mind. You will become more focused on your work after relaxing your mind. Your interests can also one day become your profession. Arbitration and Mediation have been my interests for many years and I am now able to do more work in these areas than in my engineering profession. I also enjoy it a great deal more too.

你必須維持自己的愛好和興趣，這能消除你的疲勞也能讓你放鬆。放鬆之後，你會更加專注於工作，你的興趣有一天或許會成為你的職業。仲裁和調解多年來一直是我的興趣，而現在我在這方面的工作比我工程專業上的事做得更多，我也更享受這方面的工作。

You need to love your work. If you love your work, you will drive yourself to work harder. You will engage your intellectual talent towards your work. You will learn even more and excel. You will probably define better priorities in life. You must also remember that your work actually helps you fulfill your responsibilities in life. It provides food and shelter for you and your family. It also gives you satisfaction in the accomplishments you make in life. So enjoy it.

你要熱愛你的工作，這樣才能使你更加努力，你也更能運用你的聰明才智在工作上，會學得更多，也能做得更好。你可以為人生計劃制定一個更好的優先次序，同時銘記，工作實際上是幫你去滿足和履行你人生應盡的基本責任，為你和家人提供了衣食住行的保障，同時也讓你得到一定的成就感，要學會好好享受你的工作。

Last but not the least, you must maintain good health, both physically and mentally. Things will fall apart if you do not have good health. Your desire to work will diminish when you are sick. Take time to enjoy sports, wildlife and nature, and do exercise. A good diet will also help you achieve this. You must preserve your youthfulness, happiness, health and wellbeing.

最後一點，也是非常重要的一點，你一定要保持良好的體魄和精神健康。如果你身體不好，所有事情都自然不會好。當你病倒了，你的工作慾望會減弱，所以要多些花時間去享受運動、自然、鍛鍊身體，要有良好的飲食習慣有助於你實現這一目標，保持青春、幸福和健康。

Through seven different categories of questions and answers in this book, one can have a better appreciation of the problems faced by young adults today. I have tried to provide some direct answers and they are, of course not absolute. I hope these answers can inspire young adults to think in a positive manner, or help parents' guide their children in the proper direction. I believe this book can achieve this objective. When one has a positive mind and the right attitude, one can always achieve new heights.

點
解

Attitude determines your destiny. Thank you all! Stay positive and live a happy life.

我希望通過這本書中七個類別的問題與解答，讓各位更好地解讀年輕人今天所面臨的問題。我試圖提供一些直接的答案，但這些答案不是絕對的。我希望這些答案能激勵年輕人積極地思考，或者幫助他們的父母引導孩子朝向正確的思維發展。我相信這本書能達到這個目的，當一個人有正確和積極的心態，他就可以再創高峰，態度決定命運。感謝各位，希望你們有一個積極正面和快樂的人生。

Dr. Raymond Hai Ming Leung

梁海明博士

國際專家學會出版

點　　解　Where To

作　　者：梁海明 博士（Dr. Raymond HM Leung）

版面設計：國際專家學會

漫畫設計：香港神託會培敦中學

出　　版：國際專家學會

地　　址：香港鰂魚涌華蘭路20號華蘭中心11樓05室

電　　話：2872 0060 ／ 2872 0086

傳　　真：2520 5476

印　　刷：百利美印刷有限公司

出版日期：2017年10月20日

版　　次：第一次

國際書號：ISBN 978-988-12031-0-6